TinkerActive
WORKBOOKS

1ST GRADE · MATH · AGES 6–7

by Justin Krasner

illustrated by Chad Thomas

educational consulting by Amanda Raupe

 Odd Dot · New York

Counting to 120

Read the number line aloud to get to the other side of Tinker Town. Slap your knees or clap your hands when you say each number.

12 13 14 15 16 17 18 19 20 21 22 23 24 25 26 27 28 29 30 31 32 33 34 35 36 37 38

65 66 67 68 69 70 71 72 73 74 75 76 77 78 79

Write your favorite number and count to 120 from there.

You can also:
- Count backward from 120.
- Count again, clapping twice on the tens.

109 110 111 112 113 114 115 116 117 118 119 120

Count the
windows and
write the
number.

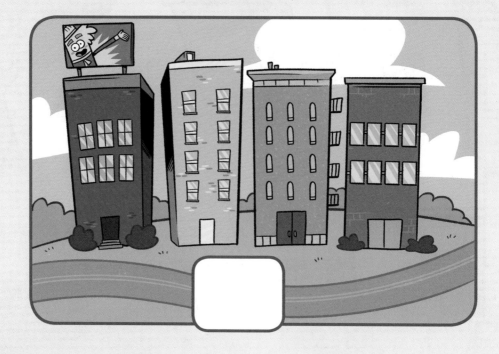

Fill in the missing numbers.

1

Counting to 120

1	2	3	4		6	7	8	9	10
			14			17		19	20
21	22			25	26		28		
		33			36		38		40
41			44			47		49	
	52				56		58	59	60
		63	64		66	67			
				75		77	78	79	
		83		85	86		88		90
91		93	94	95					100
101	102			105	106	107		109	
111	112						118		

Draw the objects missing from the park.

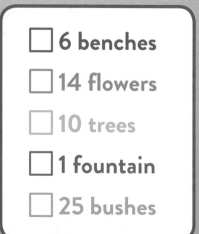

- ☐ 6 benches
- ☐ 14 flowers
- ☐ 10 trees
- ☐ 1 fountain
- ☐ 25 bushes

Connect the dots from 50 to 120.

59
58
60
62 · 57
61
63 · 56
64 · 55 · 50
66 · 65 · 54 · 51 · 52 · 53
67 · 68 · 69 · 70 · 71 · 72 · 73 · 74 · 75 · 76 · 77 · 78 · 79 · 80

120
119
102
103 · 101
104 · 100
105 · 99 · 97
106 · 98 · 96
118 · 117 · 107 · 95
116 · 108 · 94 · 93
115 · 114 · 109 · 92
113 · 112 · 111 · 110 · 90 · 91 · 89
86 · 88 · 87
83 · 81 · 82 · 84 · 85

LET'S START!

GATHER THESE TOOLS AND MATERIALS.

Dice

At least 120 blocks or snap cubes, or a box of toothpicks

10-ounce bag of mini marshmallows, modeling clay, or putty

Crayon, marker, or pencil

Paper or paper plate

Collection of your favorite snacks, like: cereal, popcorn, pretzels, nuts, etc.

LET'S TINKER!

Roll the dice to get a 2-digit number. For example, if you roll a 5 and a 4, that's 54!

Build a tower with that number of blocks, snap cubes, or toothpicks. (If using toothpicks, use the mini marshmallows, clay, or putty to hold them together.)

Continue rolling and building until you have several towers. Which tower is the tallest? Is it the tower with the most blocks? Why or why not?

LET'S MAKE: NUMBER SNACKS!

1. **Write** four numbers from 1 to 50 in different places on your paper or paper plate.

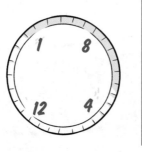

2. **Get** your favorite snacks.

3. Count out the correct number of snacks for each section.

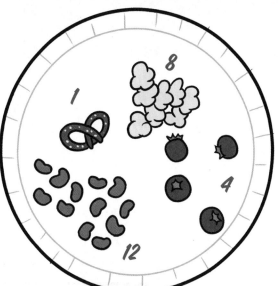

LET'S ENGINEER!

The MotMots are having a tower-building contest using snacks. The winner gets all the snacks at the end, and Frank is VERY hungry.

How can Frank build the tallest and strongest tower?

Build the tallest and strongest tower you can with your materials. **Count** the number of blocks or materials you used. **Test** it by blowing on your tower or shaking the table. What happens if you arrange your materials in another way?

PROJECT 1: DONE!
Get your sticker!

Place Value

The MotMots are taking the train to the city! Before they board, they need to pick up some supplies at the newsstand. Read each word problem aloud and answer the question.

Enid forgot her book at home.
How many books does the store have?

Frank is hungry—as usual. How many snacks are on the shelves?

Snacks

Tens	Ones

Books

Tens	Ones

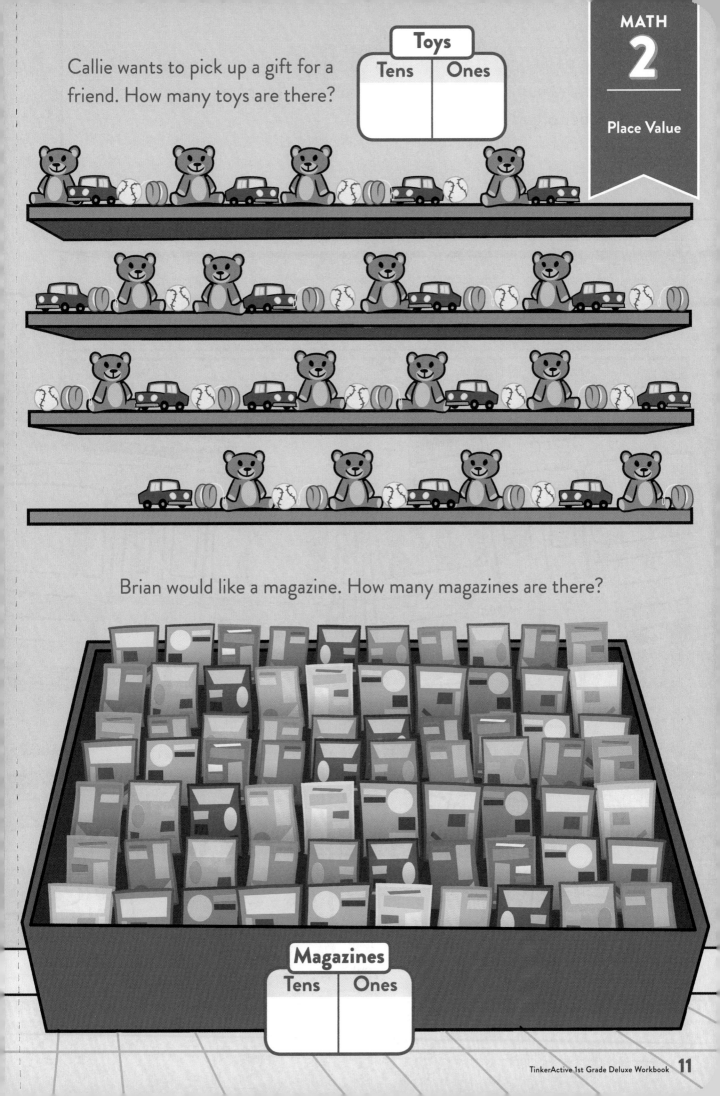

Callie wants to pick up a gift for a friend. How many toys are there?

Toys

Tens	Ones

Brian would like a magazine. How many magazines are there?

Magazines

Tens	Ones

Count the passengers in each train car aloud and circle groups of 10. Then write the number of tens and ones in each train car, as well as the total number of passengers in each train.

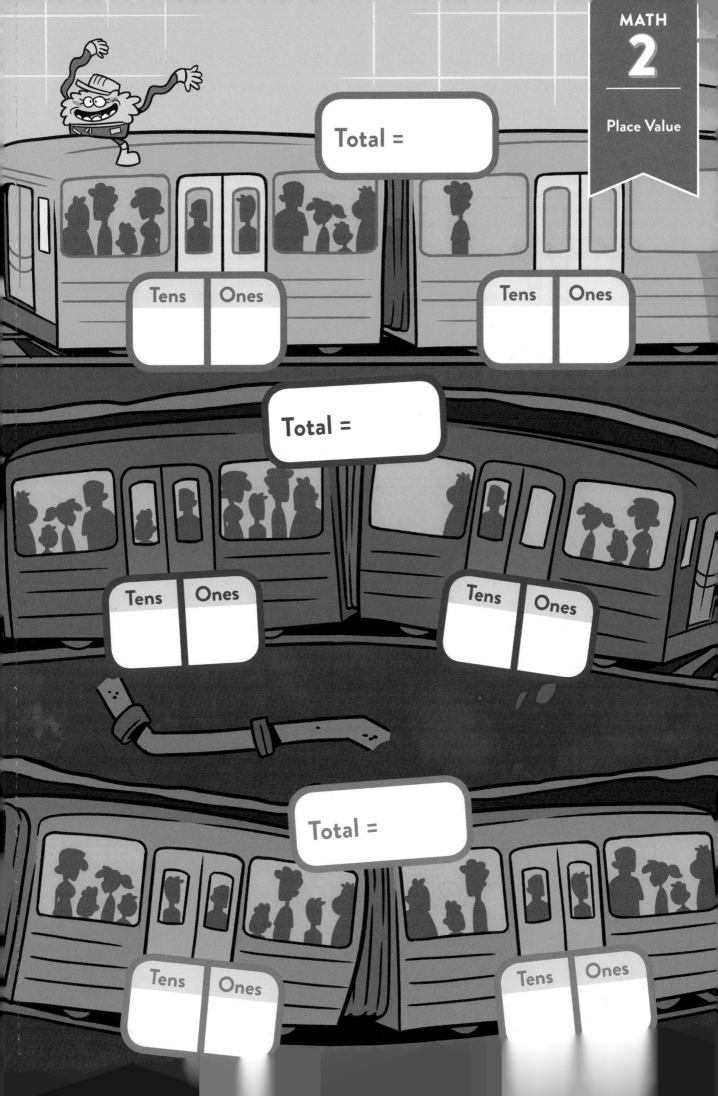

The MotMots are taking their cotton balls to the Cotton Ball Show. Fill in the place value chart to show how many tens and ones each MotMot has. Then draw the correct number of cotton balls to show the amount.

Enid is taking **34** cotton balls.

Tens	Ones
3	4

Dimitri is taking **55** cotton balls.

Tens	Ones

Amelia is taking **23** cotton balls.

Tens	Ones

Callie is taking **12** cotton balls.

Tens	Ones

Brian is taking **67** cotton balls.

Tens	Ones

Frank is taking **87** cotton balls.

Tens	Ones

LET'S START!

GATHER THESE TOOLS AND MATERIALS.

Scissors (with an adult's help)

Tape

Box of cotton swabs

Straw

Hole puncher (or ask an adult to use scissors)

3 toilet paper rolls

String

Glue

Cardboard or cereal box

Empty egg crate

Cotton balls

LET'S TINKER!

Time for target practice! **Cut** out the targets below and tape them on a wall. Then **slide** a cotton swab into your straw. **Put** the straw into your mouth, aim for the bull's-eyes, and blow! **Hit** the tens target and then the ones target. Then **combine** your score. What's the highest score you can get?

TENS

50 40 30 20

ONES

2 3 4 5

LET'S MAKE: FREIGHT TRAIN!

1. **Punch** holes through 3 toilet paper rolls (or ask an adult to poke holes using a pair of scissors).

2. **Tie** all 3 together with string to make a chain of train cars.

3. **Cut** 4 quarter-size wheels out of the cardboard or cereal box for each toilet paper train car.

4. **Glue** wheels to each train car.

5. **Decorate** your train with stickers from page 385. Then **load** your freight train with freight! How many objects can your train carry? If your train can carry more than 10 objects, how many tens and ones can it carry?

LET'S ENGINEER!

The MotMots need to take 70 cotton balls to the city for the Cotton Ball Show, and the balls must be moved in groups of ten.

How can the MotMots transport 70 cotton balls to the city?

Build a vehicle that can carry exactly 70 cotton balls. How can you keep track of how many cotton balls are in the vehicle? **Create** something that makes them easy to count.

PROJECT 2: DONE!
Get your sticker!

Comparing Two-Digit Numbers

Follow the directions.

Circle the tram with more passengers, or cross out the trams if they have an equal amount.

Circle the bush that has more berries, or cross out the bushes if they have an equal amount.

Circle the basket with more fruit, or cross out the baskets if they have an equal amount.

Draw a rectangle around the tree with fewer monkeys, or cross out the trees if they have an equal amount.

Circle the leopard with more spots, or cross out the leopards if they have an equal amount.

Draw a square around the pond with fewer fish, or cross out the ponds if they have an equal amount.

Enid must feed each alligator the larger amount of fish. Write the bigger number inside the gator's open mouth. Write the smaller number behind the gator. Then fill in the sentence and read it aloud.

43 and **52**

The alligator ate ___ fish.

67 and **76**

The alligator ate ___ fish.

53 and **21**

The alligator ate ___ fish.

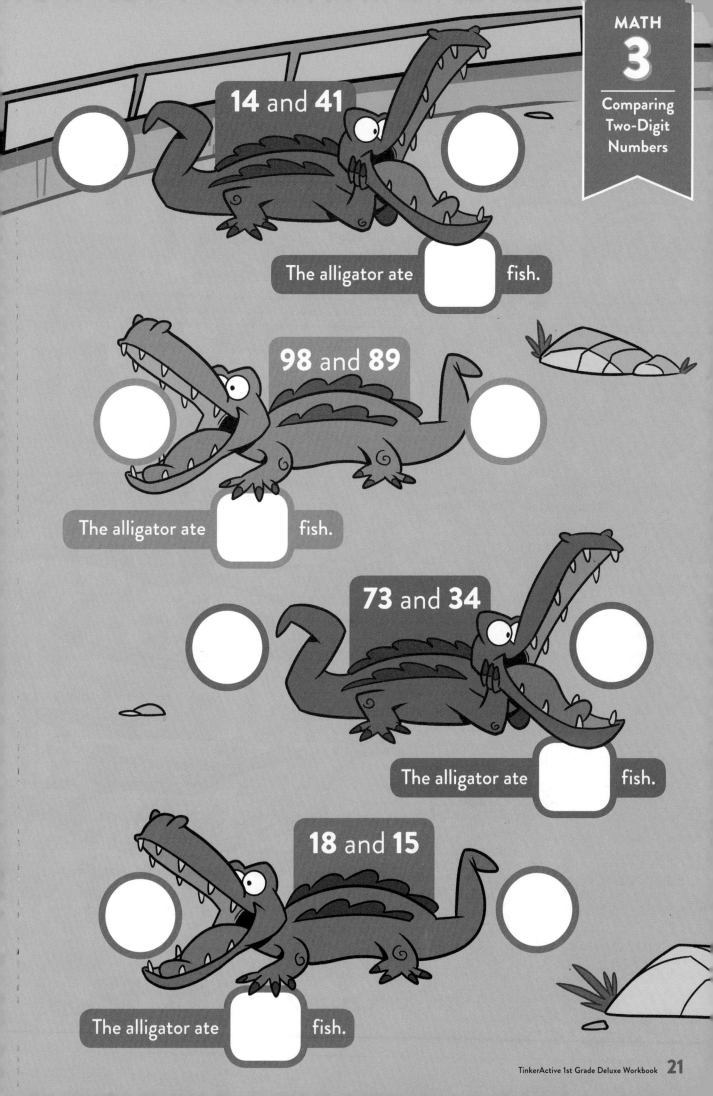

14 and **41**

The alligator ate ⬜ fish.

98 and **89**

The alligator ate ⬜ fish.

73 and **34**

The alligator ate ⬜ fish.

18 and **15**

The alligator ate ⬜ fish.

Callie and Amelia are visiting the zoo. They don't have much
time, and they want to see as many animals as possible.
Write how many animals are in each area.
Then write <, >, or = so Callie and Amelia
know which area has more animals.

If you were with Callie and Amelia, how would you walk through the zoo? Trace your finger along the path to show the way. Remember, you want to see as many animals as possible!

LET'S START!

GATHER THESE TOOLS AND MATERIALS.

3 or 4 bowls with different small items like: marbles, rice, coins, beans, buttons, etc.

Glue

Craft sticks

Crayons, markers, or paint (at least one should be green)

Scissors (with an adult's help)

Paper

Aluminum foil

3x5 cards

Tape

LET'S TINKER!

Grab a handful of objects from one bowl and another handful from another bowl.

Count how many items are in each handful. Is one handful greater than, less than, or equal to the other?

Continue comparing handfuls from different bowls. When the objects are smaller, is it easier to grab more or fewer? When the objects are larger, are you likely to grab more or fewer?

LET'S MAKE: ALLIGATOR JAWS!

1. Glue 2 craft sticks together at an angle.

2. Color them green and add an eye sticker from page 385.

3. Cut triangles out of the paper and glue them on the inside of each craft stick as teeth.

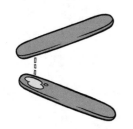

4. Look around the room. **Place** your new gator in between groups of similar objects. Remember—the gator is always looking for the bigger snack, so place the larger pile in front of her open mouth!

LET'S ENGINEER!

A pod of dolphins is swimming by the coast of Tinker Town, and the MotMots want to cheer the animals along their journey. But the boat they have can only carry 1 MotMot. They need something that can carry many more MotMots.

How can more MotMots reach the dolphins?

Build something that can carry many objects in water. **Test** your vehicle in a sink, bathtub, or large container full of water. **Fill** your vehicle with small items. How many items can it hold without sinking?

Experiment with different-size items. Can it hold more, less, or the same amount of the second material?

PROJECT 3: DONE!
Get your sticker!

Addition & Subtraction

Callie and her dog, Boxer, are walking to the mall. Callie has $20 and wants to shop at 3 stores along the way. Draw a line from the park to the mall so that Callie spends $20 at 3 stores.

AUTO

MALL

$9

CANDY

$12

BAKERY

CAFE

$19

$5

BOOKS

ICE CREAM

$3

$18

MARKET

$14

PETS

$7

Boxer ran into the bookshop and made a mess. Put the books back in place. Each bookshelf should have 10 books on the top shelf, 5 books on the middle shelf, and 20 books on the bottom shelf. Add books by drawing them and subtract books by coloring them black.

Answer each word problem.

Enid is fixing a car and needs 2 headlights, 1 door, and 2 tires.
How many new items in total does she need?

$$2+1+2=$$

Get the stickers of each item from page 385 and place them on the car.

Outside the repair shop are 5 cars, 3 trucks, and 7 bicycles.
How many vehicles are outside the shop?

There are 3 wrenches, 1 screwdriver, and 2 screws in Enid's toolbox. How many things are in her toolbox?

Some things are missing from Enid's toolbox. Draw 1 more wrench, 2 more screwdrivers, and 12 more screws. How many things do you need to draw in total?

Now that you've added more tools, how many things does Enid have in her toolbox?

Create the missing combos and write them on the menu. Include how much each costs.

OUR MENU

Cookies $1	Monday's Combo: Cookie + Peach Pie $3
Chocolate Cake $6	Tuesday's Combo:
Lemon Cake $5	Wednesday's Combo:
Blueberry Pie $4	Thursday's Combo:
Cherry Pie $3	Friday's Combo:
Peach Pie $2	

Answer each customer's question.

How much do a chocolate cake and peach pie cost together?

_____

How many different pies do you have?

_____

2 chocolate cakes, please! How much does that cost?

_____

May I please have 1 blueberry pie, 1 chocolate cake, and 1 peach pie? How much money does that cost?

_____

I'd love to have 2 lemon cakes and 1 cookie. How much is that?

_____

I'd like 1 cherry pie, 1 lemon cake, and 2 cookies. How much do I owe you?

_____

You guys make the best pies! I'll have 1 of each. How much is that altogether?

_____

LET'S START!

GATHER THESE TOOLS AND MATERIALS.

Die	Old game piece, coin, or button	Ice cream and topping pieces like: chocolate chips, walnuts, gummy bears, and cookie pieces	Bowl	Scissors (with an adult's help)
Construction paper	Pipe cleaners or straws	Tape or glue	3 vases, containers, or glasses ranging from small to medium to large	

LET'S TINKER!

Start at 1 on the game board. **Roll** the die and move your game piece that many spaces on the board. **Keep** rolling and moving your game piece until you reach 20. You must land on 20 exactly. If you roll too high, roll again.

Once you're at 20, **move** back to 1 by rolling the die and subtracting that number.

LET'S MAKE: ICE-CREAM SUNDAE!

1. **Scoop** some ice cream into a bowl.

2. **Pick** 3 toppings and decide how many of each you want (for example: 12 chocolate chips, 8 gummy bears, 5 cookie pieces, etc.).

3. How many toppings do you want in total? **Add** the number of toppings together in your head.

4. **Count** out the toppings as you add them to the sundae. Were you correct?

LET'S ENGINEER!

Brian and Frank are working at the flower shop. They need to place 10 flowers into 3 different vases: 1 small, 1 medium, and 1 large. The biggest vase should always have the most flowers, and the smallest vase should always have the least.

How many different ways can they rearrange the flowers?

Make 10 paper flowers by cutting petals out of construction paper and gluing them to pipe cleaners or colorful straws. Then **place** them in the vases—the biggest vase should always have the most flowers, and the smallest vase should always have the least. How many different arrangements can you make?

PROJECT 4: DONE!
Get your sticker!

Word Problems

Answer each word problem.

9 friends are at the jungle gym, and 10 friends are skating on the rink. How many more friends are skating than playing on the jungle gym?

4 friends are playing chess. 2 of them have to leave for a soccer game. How many friends will be left to play chess?

10 friends are skating. 7 fewer are playing catch than skating. How many friends are playing catch?

10 friends are skating. 6 have red skates. The rest have blue skates. How many skaters have blue skates?

A dog walker is walking 6 dogs. 3 are about to be picked up by their owners. How many dogs will be left?

3 swan-shaped paddleboats and 3 duck-shaped paddleboats are on the pond. How many boats are on the pond in total?

Dimitri lost his glasses and can't see a thing! Describe the picnic for him by reading the text aloud and answering each question.

6 friends are picnicking in the park. 4 more friends join them. How many friends are now at the picnic?

10 cookies and 6 brownies are on a platter. How many more cookies than brownies are on the platter?

7 candles are lit on the birthday cake. Brian blows 4 of them out. How many candles are still lit?

Frank has 15 pieces of popcorn on his plate. Amelia has 8. How many fewer pieces of popcorn does Amelia have than Frank?

4 ants are drinking the spilled juice. 8 more ants join them. How many ants are there in all?

A flock of 7 birds flies overhead. 1 bird lands by the sandwiches. How many birds are left flying overhead?

There are 14 glasses of lemonade. The friends drink 5 of them. How many glasses of lemonade are left?

There are 6 red plates. The number of blue plates is 6 more than the number of red plates. How many blue plates are there?

There are 13 large bowls and 7 small bowls. How many more large bowls are there?

Solve each word problem by using the number line. Then write the number sentence.

7 squirrels are running around the park. 2 are red. The others are gray. How many squirrels are gray?

0 1 2 3 4 (5) 6 7 8 9 10 11 12 13 14 15 16 17 18 19 20

$$7 - 2 = 5$$

10 fish poke their heads out of the pond. 4 jump back into the water. How many fish are left poking their heads out of the pond?

0 1 2 3 4 5 6 7 8 9 10 11 12 13 14 15 16 17 18 19 20

5 birds are sitting in trees. 10 birds are flying overhead. How many birds are in the park?

0 1 2 3 4 5 6 7 8 9 10 11 12 13 14 15 16 17 18 19 20

13 flowers were under the tree. Some of them were plucked. Now there are 4. How many flowers were plucked?

0 1 2 3 4 5 6 7 8 9 10 11 12 13 14 15 16 17 18 19 20

Dimitri has $12 to spend at the boathouse. Answer each question.

Dimitri wants to rent a fishing rod, a toy ship, and a paddleboat. How much money does he need to rent all 3 items?

$3

$5

$7

Does he have enough money?

If not, how much more money does Dimitri need?

Can he rent more than 1 toy ship?

Can Dimitri rent more than 1 paddleboat?

Can he rent more than 1 fishing rod?

How many fishing rods, toy ships, or paddleboats would you rent with $12? Write the item or items.

LET'S START!

GATHER THESE TOOLS AND MATERIALS.

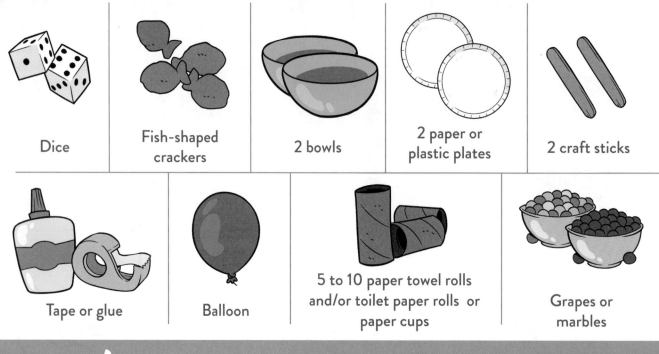

Dice

Fish-shaped crackers

2 bowls

2 paper or plastic plates

2 craft sticks

Tape or glue

Balloon

5 to 10 paper towel rolls and/or toilet paper rolls or paper cups

Grapes or marbles

LET'S TINKER!

Go fish! **Roll** the dice, add the numbers, and pour the corresponding number of fish-shaped crackers into the first bowl.

Roll the dice again and pour the corresponding number of crackers into the second bowl. How many more or fewer crackers are in the second bowl? How many crackers are there in total?

Eat a few crackers from each bowl. Now how many more or fewer crackers are there in the second bowl? How many crackers are there in total?

LET'S MAKE: PADDLE PLAY!

1. Tape or glue the top of a craft stick to the bottom of a paper or plastic plate to create a paddle.

2. Make 1 more paddle.

3. Blow up and tie a balloon.

4. Get a partner and play. **Hit** the balloon back and forth with the paddles so the balloon doesn't touch the ground. Starting from zero, **add** 1 point to your score each time you knock the balloon back to your partner.

If the balloon hits the ground, **subtract** 3 points and start counting again from your new number. If you don't reach 3 points before the balloon hits the ground, **start** again from zero. Can you get all the way to 20?

LET'S ENGINEER!

The MotMots love to snack on grapes. They can't get enough! But the grapes are all the way on top of the counter, and they're busy playing on the kitchen floor.

How can the MotMots get the grapes from the counter to the floor?

Design a solution using your materials. Which materials did you choose? Why?

Test your solution with grapes or marbles.

Count each kind of material, then add them together. How many materials did you use in all?

PROJECT 5: DONE!
Get your sticker!

Addition & Subtraction Equations

You are a food critic! Circle the thumbs-up next to the equations that are true and the thumbs-down next to the equations that are false.

$6 - 4 = 3$

$8 = 6 + 2$

$7 + 3 = 10$

$5 + 2 = 7$

$8 - 3 = 5$

$12 = 6 + 6$

$9 + 5 = 14$

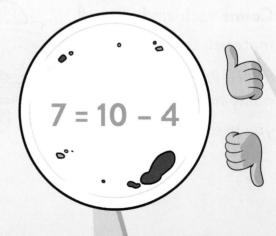

$7 = 10 - 4$

11 + 3 = 3 + 11

6 − 3 = 3 + 6

3 + 4 = 3 + 5

5 + 4 = 4 + 5

Fix each false number sentence. Fill in the blanks to write a new true sentence below.

6 + 4 ≠ 2

6 + 4 = ☐

4 + 6 = ☐

☐ − 6 = 4

☐ − 4 = 6

7 ≠ 11 − 3

☐ = 11 − 3

3 = 11 − ☐

☐ + 3 = 11

3 + ☐ = 11

12 − 3 ≠ 8

12 − ☐ = 8

12 − 8 = ☐

8 + ☐ = 12

☐ + 8 = 12

Use the numbers at the top of each menu to fill in the blanks. Say each number sentence aloud as you fill it in.

4, 9, 5

$4 + \boxed{} = \boxed{}$

$\boxed{} - 5 = \boxed{}$

$\boxed{} + \boxed{} = 9$

$9 - \boxed{} = \boxed{}$

2, 10, 8

$\boxed{} + 8 = \boxed{}$

$10 - \boxed{} = \boxed{}$

$\boxed{} + 2 = \boxed{}$

$\boxed{} - \boxed{} = 8$

3, 4, 7

$\boxed{} + \boxed{} = 7$

$\boxed{} - 3 = \boxed{}$

$4 + \boxed{} = \boxed{}$

$7 - \boxed{} = \boxed{}$

Amelia must figure out which containers don't have an equal amount of ingredients and refill them.

Cross out the containers that are not equal.

$6 + 3 = 6 + 4$

$2 + 9 = 9 + 2$

$3 + 7 = 7 + 1$

$4 + 8 = 8 + 4$

Fill in the missing number to keep the trays balanced.

$3 + 4 = 4 + \boxed{}$

$7 + 3 = \boxed{} + 7$

$\boxed{} + 2 = 2 + 8$

$10 + 1 = 7 + \boxed{}$

$8 = \boxed{} - 2$

CAFE

$5 - 2 = 4 - \boxed{}$

$9 + 6 + 1 = \boxed{} + 8$

$10 + 7 = \boxed{} + 5 + 6$

$4 + 2 + 5 = 10 + \boxed{}$

$8 + 3 + 2 = 9 + \boxed{}$

$7 - \boxed{} = 9 - 6$

$\boxed{} + 3 = 9 - 2$

LET'S START!

GATHER THESE TOOLS AND MATERIALS.

Sliced fruit
(apples, oranges, or bananas)

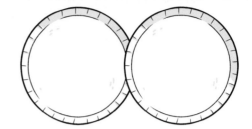

2 plates

Pack of stackable, rimmed
Styrofoam cups

Marker

LET'S TINKER!

Place some slices of fruit on 2 plates. Do both plates have the same amount of fruit slices? If not, **make** them equal by transferring fruit. Then **snack** away! **Keep** each plate equal to the other while you eat the fruit.

LET'S MAKE: MATH MACHINE!

1. Get 5 Styrofoam cups.

2. Write the numbers zero to 20 with a marker along the rim of 3 cups.

3. **Write** a plus, minus, and equal sign on the rim of 2 cups (spaced far apart from one another).

4. **Stack** your cups by sandwiching the plus, minus, and equal sign cups between the zero to 20 cups.

5. **Turn** the cups to make a true number sentence or turn the cups randomly and say whether or not the equations are true.

1 2 3 4 5
— + =
6 7 8 9 10
+ = —
9 10 11 12

LET'S ENGINEER!

Enid, Amelia, and Dimitri want to be detectives. But they need a secret way of communicating with one another.

How can they write and read messages to one another without the other MotMots knowing?

HINT:
You'll need more cups than you used for your math machine.

Build something similar to your math machine that could work as a secret-message decoder.

Assign each letter of the alphabet to a number to create a secret code.

PROJECT 6: DONE!
Get your sticker!

Determining Unknown Numbers

Fill in the missing number on each poster.

WANTED

$8 - 3 = \boxed{}$

WANTED

$14 - \boxed{} = 7$

WANTED

$18 = \boxed{} + 5$

WANTED

$9 + \boxed{} = 16$

WANTED

$\boxed{} = 10 - 4$

WANTED

$10 = \boxed{} - 5$

WANTED

$3 + 9 = \boxed{}$

WANTED

$\boxed{} + 7 = 10$

WANTED

$\boxed{} + 8 = 20$

WANTED

$9 - 6 = \boxed{}$

WANTED

It's Giving Day in Tinker Town! The MotMots are giving and receiving gifts all day. Read each word problem and fill in the blanks.

Callie had 12 flowers. Now she has 5. Callie gave away _____ flowers!

Brian had 10 crayons. Now he has _____. Brian gave away 5 crayons!

Frank had 9 cookies. Now he has 12. Frank was given _____ more cookies.

Dimitri had 7 balloons. Now he has _____. Dimitri was given 4 more balloons!

Enid had _____ stuffed animals. Now she has 14. Enid was given 6 stuffed animals!

Amelia had _____ baseball cards. Now she has 10. Amelia gave away 2 baseball cards!

It's snack time for the dogs. Help feed them by following the instructions.

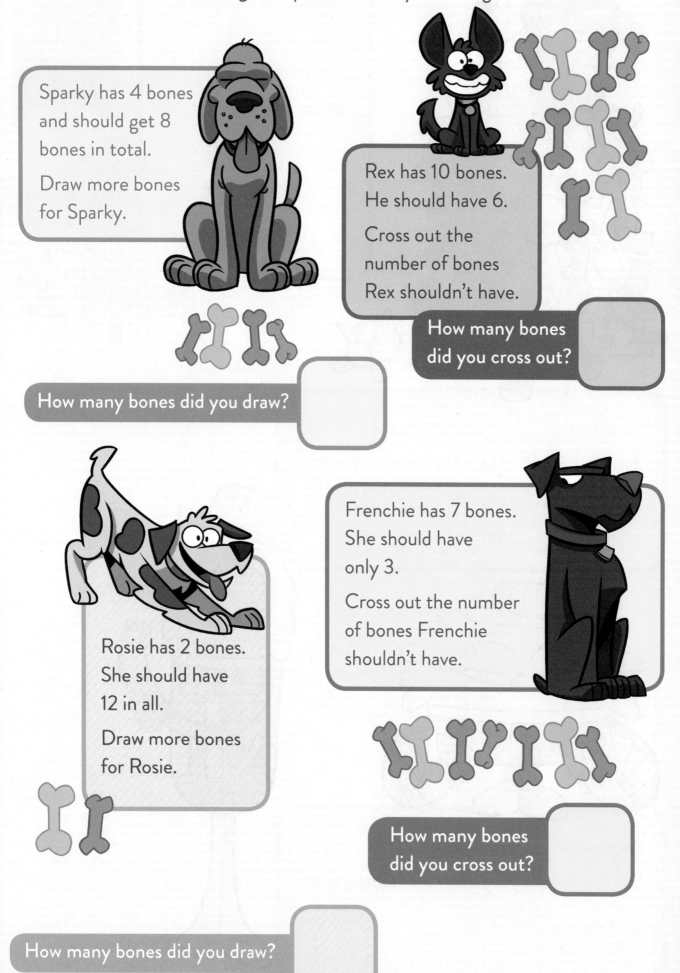

Sparky has 4 bones and should get 8 bones in total.

Draw more bones for Sparky.

Rex has 10 bones. He should have 6.

Cross out the number of bones Rex shouldn't have.

How many bones did you cross out?

How many bones did you draw?

Rosie has 2 bones. She should have 12 in all.

Draw more bones for Rosie.

Frenchie has 7 bones. She should have only 3.

Cross out the number of bones Frenchie shouldn't have.

How many bones did you cross out?

How many bones did you draw?

Write the missing number
in the number bond.
Then fill in the number
sentences.

5
⬤ **2**

[ ] + 2 = 5

5 − 2 = [ ]

2 + [ ] = 5

5 − [ ] = 2

9
⬤ **4**

[ ] + [ ] = [ ]

[ ] − [ ] = [ ]

[ ] + [ ] = [ ]

[ ] − [ ] = [ ]

10
6 ⬤

[ ] + [ ] = [ ]

[ ] − [ ] = [ ]

[ ] + [ ] = [ ]

[ ] − [ ] = [ ]

12
7 ⬤

[ ] + [ ] = [ ]

[ ] − [ ] = [ ]

[ ] + [ ] = [ ]

[ ] − [ ] = [ ]

Scissors (with an adult's help)

Dice

Construction paper

Clothes hanger

String

Small weighted objects

2 small buckets with handles of equal size or cups

LET'S TINKER!

Cut out the birds and the branch below. **Roll** the dice and add the numbers together—that is the number of birds that should be on the tree. For example, if you roll a 5 and 2, put 7 birds on the tree. How many birds did you put on the tree?

Keep rolling and trying new combinations.

LET'S MAKE: DOT ART!

1. **Fill** in the number sentences.

10
7

☐ + ☐ = ☐

☐ − ☐ = ☐

☐ + ☐ = ☐

☐ − ☐ = ☐

2. **Sticker** the dots from page 385 on construction paper to represent your answers.

'Art Dot'
Enid Motmot

LET'S ENGINEER!

Frank was working at the grocery store. He was in charge of weighing the fruit. He carried a HUGE watermelon over to the scale, dropped it, and SMASH—it was so heavy it broke his scale!

How can Frank make a new scale?

Build a scale with your materials. When you're done, **place** a small handful of items on each side of the scale.

Balance the scale by adding or subtracting items from one side. How many items did you have to add or subtract to make both sides of the scale equal?

PROJECT 7: DONE!
Get your sticker!

Place Value & Addition

Write the number that is 10 less and the number that is 10 more.

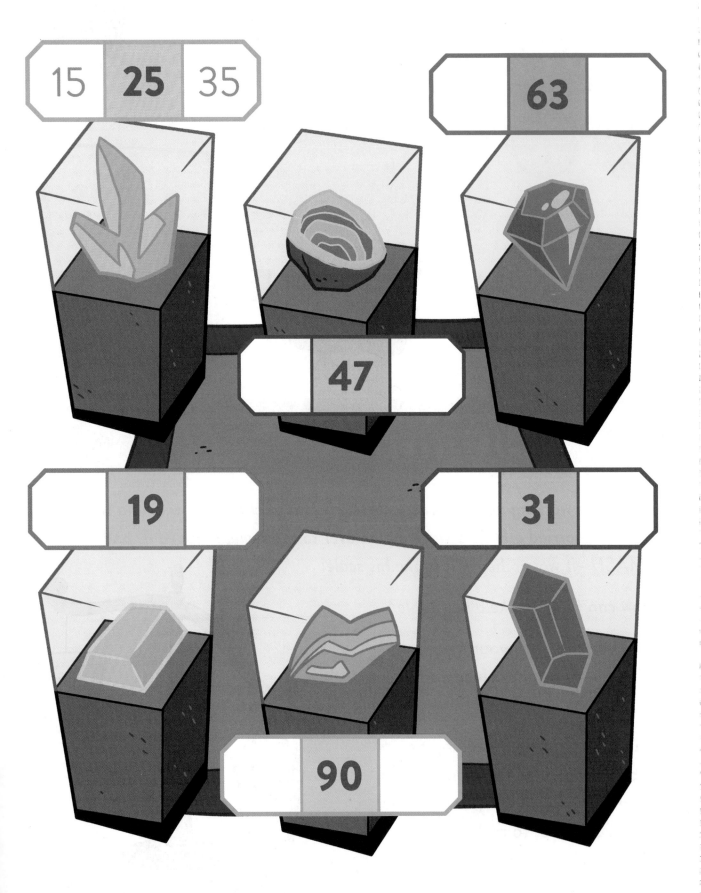

| 15 | **25** | 35 |

| | **63** | |

| | 47 | |

| **19** | |

| **31** | |

| | **90** | |

Follow the directions.

26

36

56

45

Circle the number that is **10 less** than **46**.

107

37

27

7

Circle the number that is **10 more** than **17**.

15

43

63

35

Circle the number that is **10 less** than **53**.

87

99

97

79

Circle the number that is **10 more** than **89**.

Each display case has bundles of 10 fossils as well as single fossils.
Write the total number of items in each display case.

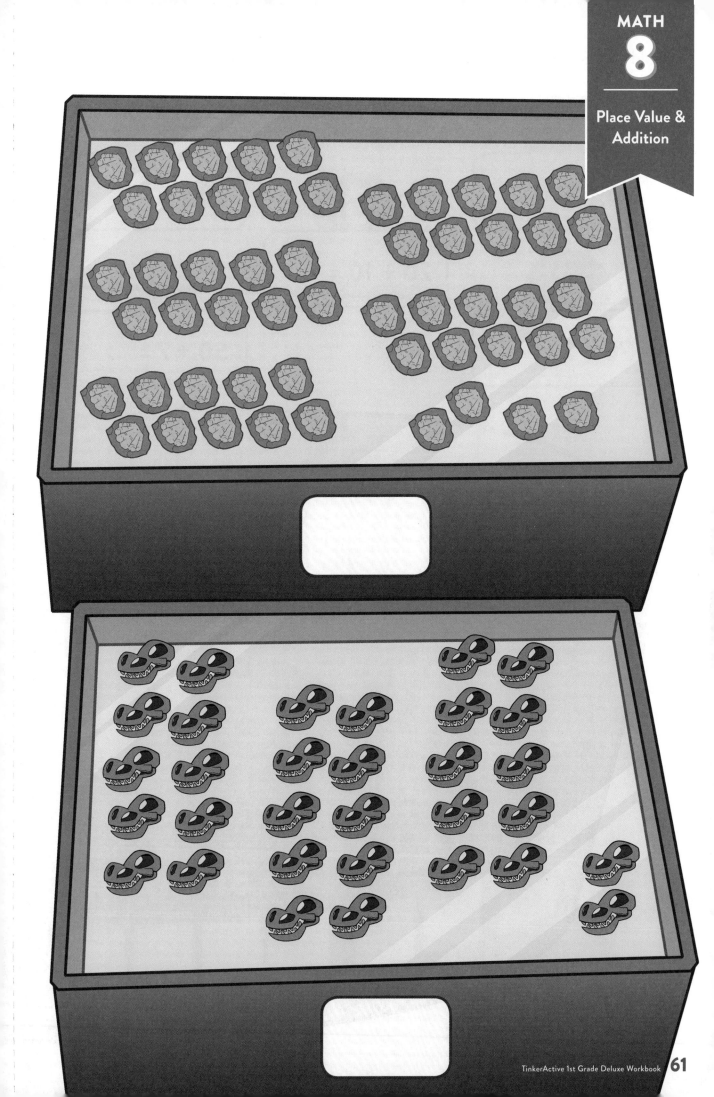

Add to get the letters. Then decode the message on the sarcophagus.

I
40 + 8 =

S
20 + 10 =

J
30 + 6 =

G
70 + 2 =

P
50 + 7 =

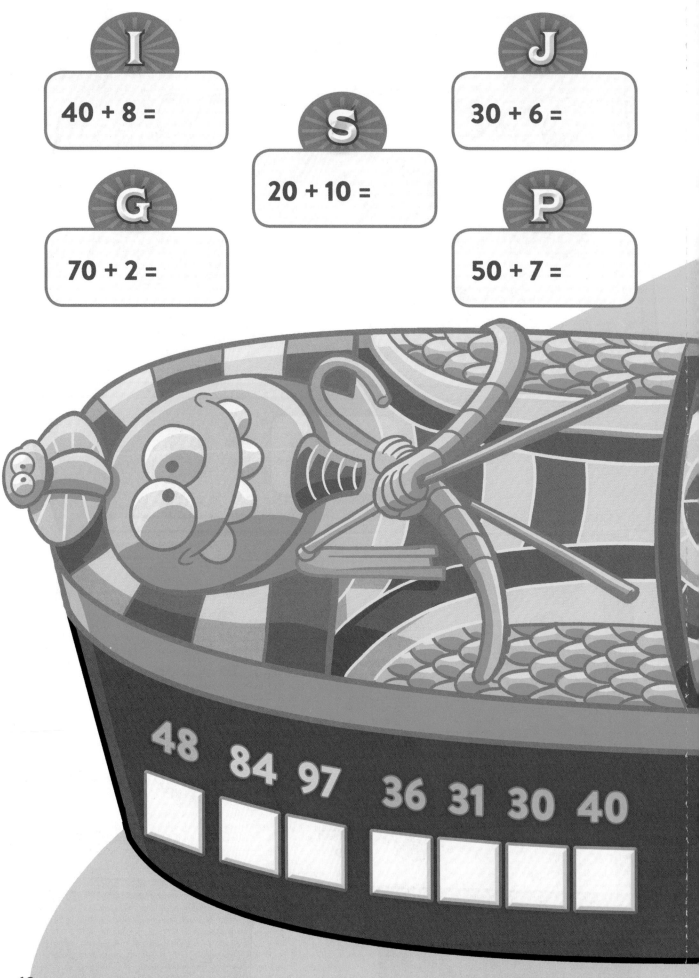

48   84   97   36   31   30   40

N 5 + 90 =

U 1 + 30 =

A 80 + 4 =

M 90 + 7 =

T 10 + 30 =

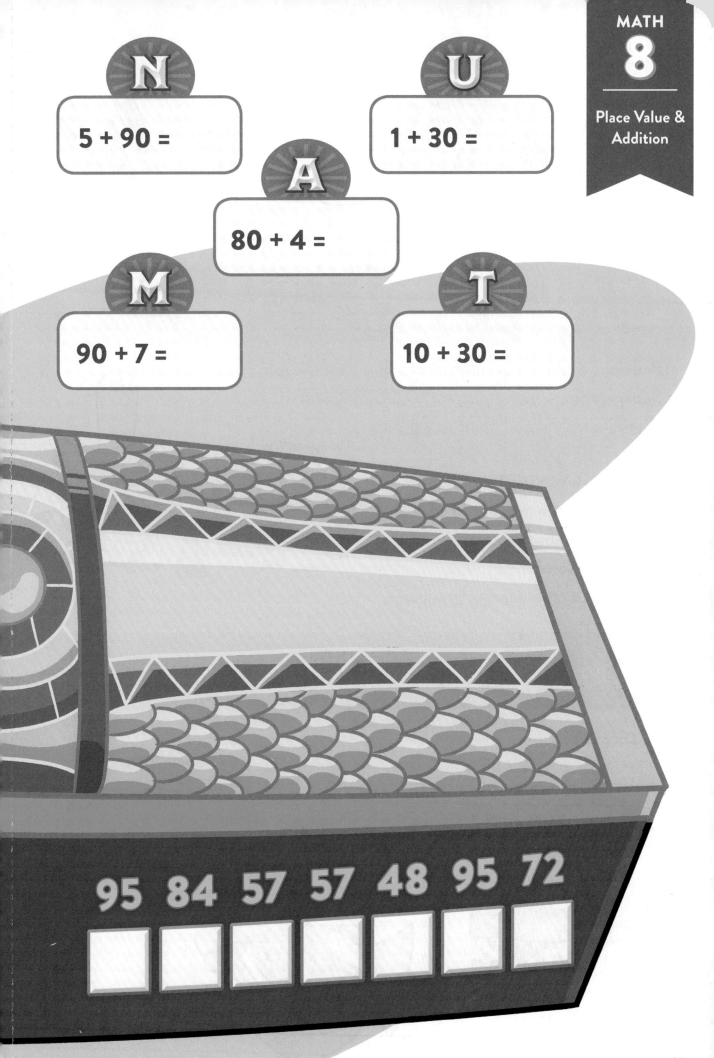

95 84 57 57 48 95 72

LET'S START!

GATHER THESE TOOLS AND MATERIALS.

A box of 100 to 1,000 craft sticks or cotton swabs

Construction paper

Glue

Scissors
(with an adult's help)

4 clothespins

LET'S TINKER!

Pour out a pile of 100 craft sticks or cotton swabs.
Separate them into groups of 10, 20, 30, and 40.
Close your eyes and point to a group.
Open your eyes and—without counting—what is 10 more or 10 less than the number of sticks or cotton swabs in that group?
Too easy? **Combine** groups together to create larger groups.

LET'S MAKE: DINOSAUR FOSSILS!

1. Cut out the dinosaur skulls.

2. Glue craft sticks or cotton swabs onto construction paper to build your own dinosaur fossils.

3. How many craft sticks or cotton swabs did you use to make the legs? How many did you use for the torso? How many for the neck? **Count** each segment. Then **add** up the total.

LET'S ENGINEER!

The MotMots were so excited to go to the natural history museum and see the giant standing dinosaur fossil. But when they arrived, they discovered that the fossil had been removed for cleaning!

How can the MotMots make their own standing dinosaur fossil?

Use craft sticks and clothespins to build a dinosaur fossil that can stand up like the ones in a natural history museum.

Count the number of craft sticks you used.

Now **count** the number of clothespins. How many craft sticks and clothespins did you use in all?

PROJECT 8: DONE!
Get your sticker!

Place Value & Subtraction

Look at the hundreds chart. Then trace the multiples of 10 while reading them aloud.

1	2	3	4	5	6	7	8	9	10
11	12	13	14	15	16	17	18	19	20
21	22	23	24	25	26	27	28	29	30
31	32	33	34	35	36	37	38	39	40
41	42	43	44	45	46	47	48	49	50
51	52	53	54	55	56	57	58	59	60
61	62	63	64	65	66	67	68	69	70
71	72	73	74	75	76	77	78	79	80
81	82	83	84	85	86	87	88	89	90
91	92	93	94	95	96	97	98	99	100

Fill in the missing numbers. Use the hundreds chart to guide you.

60 – 40 =

30 – 10 =

50 – 40 =

70 – 20 =

90 – 60 =

80 – 30 =

Connect the stars from 100 to zero.
Circle each multiple of 10 as you go!

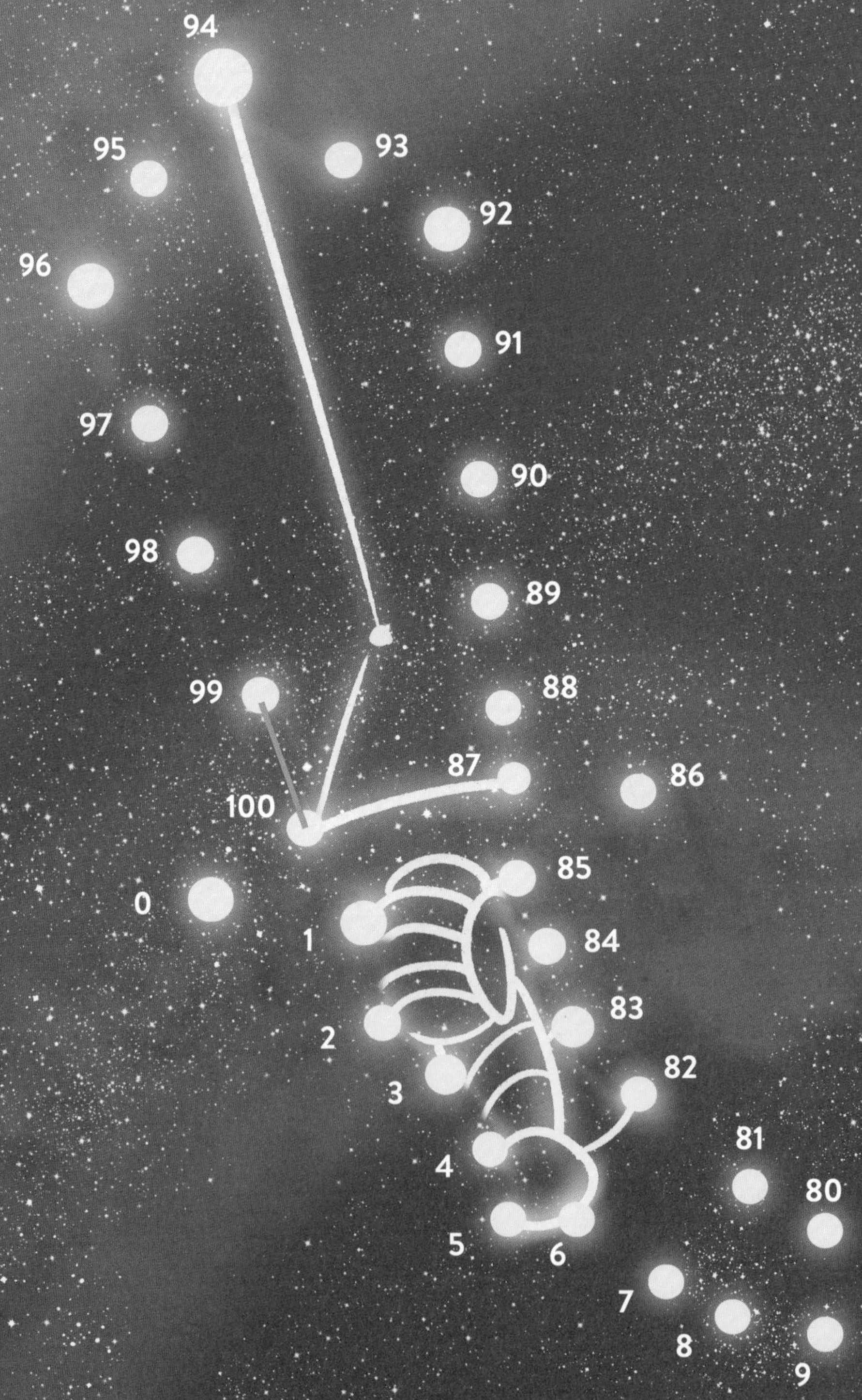

94

95

93

92

96

91

97

90

98

89

99

88

87

86

100

85

0

84

1

83

2

82

3

81

4

80

5

6

7

8

9

Use the number line to show the difference.

$90 - 10 = 80$

0 10 20 30 40 50 60 70 80 90 100

$20 - 10 =$

0 10 20 30 40 50 60 70 80 90 100

$60 - 10 =$

0 10 20 30 40 50 60 70 80 90 100

$70 - 20 =$

0 10 20 30 40 50 60 70 80 90 100

$50 - 30 =$

0 10 20 30 40 50 60 70 80 90 100

50 − 40 =

⟵ 0 10 20 30 40 50 60 70 80 90 100 ⟶

70 − 60 =

⟵ 0 10 20 30 40 50 60 70 80 90 100 ⟶

90 − 40 =

⟵ 0 10 20 30 40 50 60 70 80 90 100 ⟶

70 − 30 =

⟵ 0 10 20 30 40 50 60 70 80 90 100 ⟶

80 − 20 =

⟵ 0 10 20 30 40 50 60 70 80 90 100 ⟶

LET'S START!

GATHER THESE TOOLS AND MATERIALS.

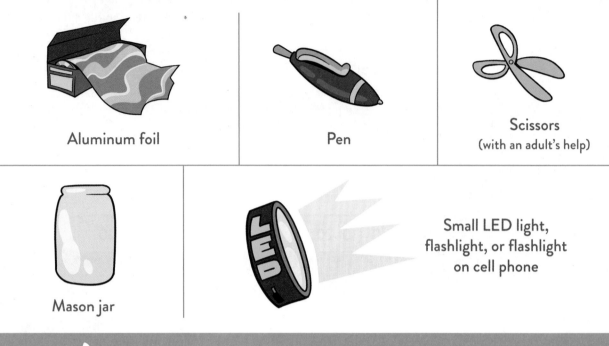

Aluminum foil

Pen

Scissors
(with an adult's help)

Mason jar

Small LED light,
flashlight, or flashlight
on cell phone

LET'S TINKER!

Poke 50 holes in a large sheet of aluminum foil with a pen, clustering them in groups of 10.
Cover some up with your hand. How many groups of 10 are there now? Keep **moving** your hand around to cover different amounts of groups.

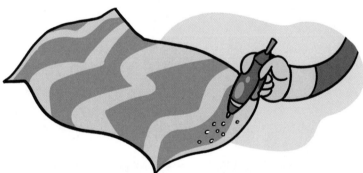

LET'S MAKE: PLANETARIUM!

1. Cut a rectangular strip of aluminum foil large enough to cover the entire inside of the jar.

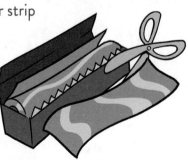

2. Poke 90 holes in groups of 10 with a pen.

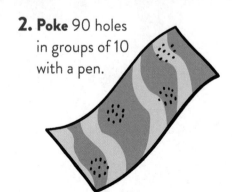

3. Line the jar with the foil.

4. Place the LED light inside and cover with the lid.

5. Turn the lights off and watch your sky light up!

LET'S ENGINEER!

The MotMots love their homemade planetariums. They use them as night-lights and keep them right by their beds. But they are so bright! They want to see some stars, but not so many that they can't fall asleep at night.

How can the MotMots block some of the light coming through their planetariums?

Block some light so that only 70 points of light shine through your planetarium. Next, **try** only 50 stars. How about 20? **Try** different amounts until you have the perfect amount of light for a night-light.

PROJECT 9: DONE!
Get your sticker!

Measuring & Comparing Lengths

Color the tallest MotMot in each row **green**. Color the shortest MotMot in each row **red**. Color the midsize MotMot **blue**.

Color the tallest building in each row **green**. Color the shortest building in each row **red**. Color the midsize building **blue**.

Line up paper clips to measure each length and answer each question.

Who is shorter, **Dimitri** or **Brian**?

Who has the shorter arm, **Brian** or **Callie**?

Callie

Dimitri

Brian

Who has the longer leg,
Brian or **Amelia**?

Who has the longer arm,
Callie or **Dimitri**?

Amelia

Choose one of the materials below and circle it. Then, get the object and use it to measure each illustrated object on page 79. Last, record your measurement on the chart.

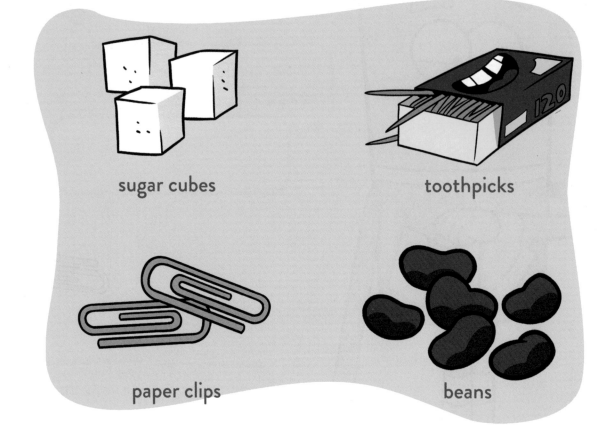

sugar cubes

toothpicks

paper clips

beans

Object	Measurement
Pencil	
Spoon	
Cup	
Sock	

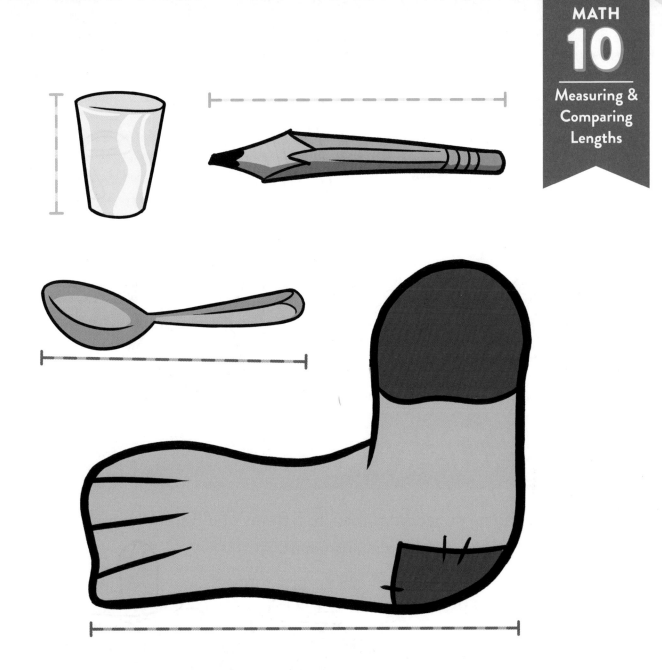

List the items from longest to shortest.

1.	
2.	
3.	
4.	

Do you have any of these objects in your home? Try measuring them!

LET'S START!

GATHER THESE TOOLS AND MATERIALS.

Long items like:
jump ropes, shoelaces, or belts

4–8 straws

Scissors
(with an adult's help)

Tape

Paper clips

Suitcase or bag

LET'S TINKER!

Search your home or backyard for 3 to 5 items of different lengths, such as a jump rope, a shoelace, and a belt.

Place your objects on a floor or table.

Put them in order from shortest to longest.

Can you **find** other objects that are even shorter or longer?

LET'S MAKE: STRAW FLUTE!

1. Cut straws into different lengths.

2. Put the pieces next to one another from shortest to longest.

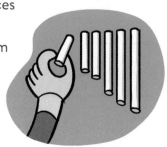

3. Tape them together in a row.

4. Blow back and forth to make some music.

LET'S ENGINEER!

Frank is going on a vacation. He wants to bring lots of stuff—his swimsuit, a tennis racket, his favorite stuffed animal, a pillow, and more. But everything he wants to bring is a different size.

How can Frank find out if something will fit in his suitcase?

Measure the inside of a suitcase or bag with a paper clip. Now **find** some objects around your house that you would pack for a vacation. Using the same paper clip, **measure** the length of each item.

Will it fit inside the suitcase? **Try** packing it inside. Were you right?

PROJECT 10: DONE!
Get your sticker!

Telling & Writing Time

Read each clock. Then draw a line to match the times on the clocks.

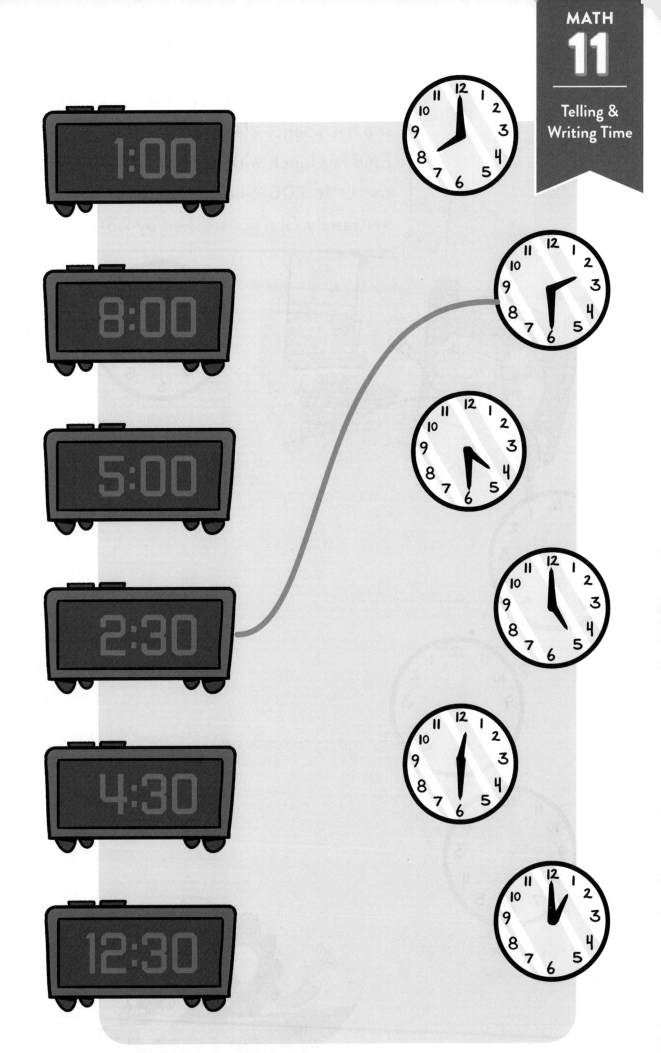

Read the story aloud. Then draw the time on the clock and complete each sentence.

Enid wakes up at 6:30. She eats breakfast at 7:00 and gets to school by 8:00. At 10:30, she has science class—her favorite. At 12:00, Enid has lunch with her friends. She plays soccer at 3:00. She eats dinner at 5:00 with her family. She goes to bed by 7:30.

Enid wakes up at

_____ : _____ .

She eats breakfast at _____ .

Enid gets to school at _____ .

She has science class at

_____ .

Enid has lunch at _____ .

She plays soccer at

_____ .

She eats dinner at _____ .

She goes to bed by

_____ .

Read the clock. Then write the time.

Read the clock. Then write the time.

LET'S START!

GATHER THESE TOOLS AND MATERIALS.

Clock or watch

Pencil, crayon, or marker

Paper

Cardboard box or construction paper

Scissors
(with an adult's help)

Hole puncher
(or ask an adult to use scissors)

Paper fastener or paper clip

LET'S TINKER!

Keep a time log of your day like Enid did on pages 84 and 85. First, **write** what time you wake up. Then, **write** all of your activities during the day and when you did them. Last, **write** what time you go to bed.

WAKE UP

EAT BREAKFAST

GO TO SCHOOL

GO TO BED

LET'S MAKE: CARDBOARD CLOCK!

1. Cut a circle and 2 clock hands (one shorter than the other) out of a cardboard box or construction paper.

2. Punch a hole through one end of the hands and the middle of the clock.

3. Attach the hands to the clock with a paper fastener or paper clip.

4. Add numbers and decorate.

5. Set your clock! **Show** what time it is.

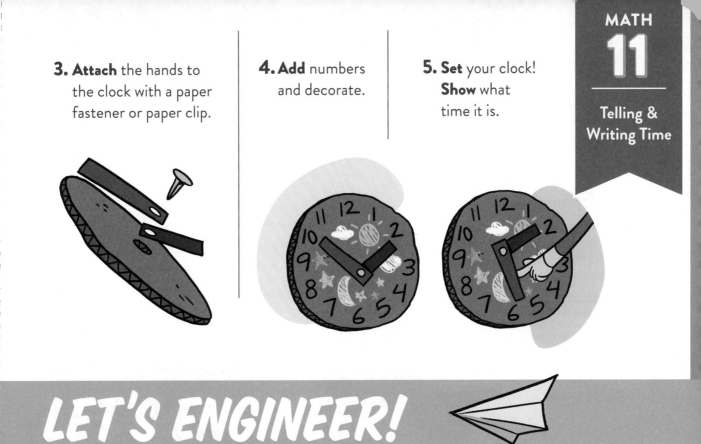

LET'S ENGINEER!

Today is Tinker Town's paper airplane contest! Amelia won the contest last year. She folded and flew a paper airplane in under 6 minutes! She wants to be even faster this year.

How can Amelia beat her record?

Using an analog or digital clock, **time** yourself as you fold and fly a paper airplane. **Read** the time when you start folding your plane. Then **read** the time when your plane lands on the ground. How many minutes passed?

Were you faster than 6 minutes? If not, **try** again, or try a different airplane design. How long does each design take to make? Can you beat Amelia's record?

PROJECT 11: DONE!
Get your sticker!

Data

Tally the number of MotMots rooting for each team.
Then write the total number of fans for each team.

Fans	Tally	Total
Blue Team Fans	|||| |||| |||| ||||	20
Red Team Fans		

Tally the number of MotMots with and without megaphones.
Then write the total for each group.

Fans	Tally	Total
With Megaphones		
Without Megaphones		

How many fans are there in all?

At the pep rally, the MotMots have worn the jerseys of their favorite sport. Tally each MotMot's favorite sport as you say them aloud.

Sport	Tally
Baseball	
Basketball	
Football	

Use the chart on the previous page to answer the questions.

How many MotMots chose basketball as their favorite sport?	
How many MotMots chose football as their favorite sport?	
How many MotMots chose baseball as their favorite sport?	
How many more MotMots chose basketball than baseball?	
How many MotMots were asked about their favorite sport?	
Which sport is the most MotMots' favorite?	

Ask your friends and family what their favorite sports are and make your own chart! How many people do you know who are fans of basketball, football, and baseball? What about other sports?

Tally each MotMot's snack. Then use the chart to answer the questions.

Snacks	Tally	Total
Pizza		
Nachos		
Pretzels		

How many fans are eating snacks?	
How many fans are eating nachos?	
How many more fans are eating pizza than pretzels?	
What is the total number of fans who are eating pizza and nachos?	
Which food is the most popular?	
Which food is the least popular?	
Which 2 snacks did a total of 12 fans eat?	

LET'S START!

GATHER THESE TOOLS AND MATERIALS.

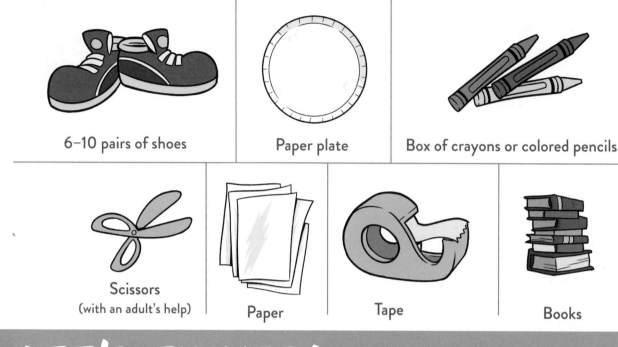

6–10 pairs of shoes

Paper plate

Box of crayons or colored pencils

Scissors
(with an adult's help)

Paper

Tape

Books

LET'S TINKER!

Gather shoes from around your home. **Sort** them into 3 groups.

How did you sort your shoes? By color? By size? By season?
How many shoes are in each group?

Sort them in another way.
How many shoes are in each group now?
How many ways can you sort the shoes?

LET'S MAKE: WEATHER WHEEL!

1. **Divide** a
   paper plate
   into 5 equal
   sections.

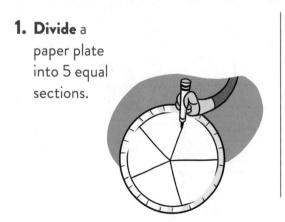

2. **Draw** an image for a kind of weather
   in each section: sunny, cloudy, rainy,
   windy, and snowy.

3. Cut out a paper arrow.

4. Tape the arrow on the weather for the day.

5. Tally the weather for 1 week. At the end of the week, how many days were in each category?

LET'S ENGINEER!

Enid loves to read! She has a big book collection—and it's growing! Her collection is growing so fast that her bookshelf is a mess! When she wants to find a certain kind of book, it's impossible.

How can Enid organize her books so she can easily find the type of book she wants?

Look at the books in your home. **Sort** the books so it's easy to find one that you like.

What categories matter to you? Subjects like animals and sports? Or authors like Dr. Seuss?

Sort the books into 3 categories. If you wanted to tell someone else about your books, how could you show the groups and number of books?

PROJECT 12: DONE!
Get your sticker!

Shapes

Use the key to color the campsite.

Key

- **Circles: Green**
- **Squares: Red**
- **Rectangles: Blue**
- **Triangles: Orange**
- **Hexagons: Yellow**

Circle the closed shapes. Cross out the open shapes.
Then draw a closed-shaped and an open-shaped constellation.

Use the key to color the shapes in the constellation.

Key

All shapes without corners: blue

All 3-sided shapes: brown

All 4-sided shapes: orange

Read the text aloud. Then draw the shape and write the name.

I have zero straight sides and zero corners. What shape am I?

_____

I have 3 straight sides and 3 corners. What shape am I?

_____

I have 4 straight sides and 4 corners. What shape am I?

_____

I have 6 straight sides and 6 corners. What shape am I?

_____

Read about 3-dimensional shapes.

All rectangular prisms have 6 faces.

All cylinders are solid shapes.

All spheres are round.

All pyramids are made of triangles.

Then fill in the blanks in the story with words from the box.

| curved | triangles | rectangular prism |
| sphere | cylinder | pyramid | six |

The MotMots went camping for Enid's birthday! Enid brought a

book to read by the campfire. The book was a

_____ and had _____ faces.

For lunch, Frank packed his favorite—a giant can of tomato soup. The can was a

_____—just like the mugs they used to drink it.

After lunch, the MotMots played baseball. The baseball bat was

a cylinder, but the baseball was a _____. The sides of the

baseball and baseball bat were _____. Amelia hit a home run! At night,

the MotMots slept in a tent. It was in the shape of a _____.

The sides of their tent were shaped like _____. Before they went to

bed, they watched the sky. The moon looked like half a sphere, and Enid even saw

a shooting star. Enid had a very happy birthday!

LET'S START!

6 to 8 toothpicks, straws, cotton swabs, or craft sticks

10-ounce bag of mini marshmallows, modeling clay, or putty

Construction paper

Scissors
(with an adult's help)

Tape

LET'S TINKER!

Look around the room you're in. What shapes can you find?

Count each type of shape. Are there more of a certain shape than another? Why do you think that is?

LET'S MAKE: STICK SHAPES!

1. **Make** 2 closed shapes with the toothpicks, straws, cotton swabs, or craft sticks. **Name** each shape and describe it. What makes it the shape it is?

2. **Use** mini marshmallows, modeling clay, or putty to connect your shapes and create a 3-dimensional shape. What shape is it now? **Describe** it.

LET'S ENGINEER!

Amelia and Callie are designing a new building, and they want to stack one shape for the whole thing.

How can Amelia and Callie choose the best shape for stacking?

Cut out 15 equal-size strips of construction paper. **Fold** each strip and tape it together into a shape. **Try** folding a few different shapes. **Stack** them any way you want to build a structure.

Test how strong your structure is by placing different items on top of it. Do some shapes create stronger structures than others?

PROJECT 13: DONE!
Get your sticker!

Composing Shapes

Build a new neighborhood in Tinker Town by drawing shapes.

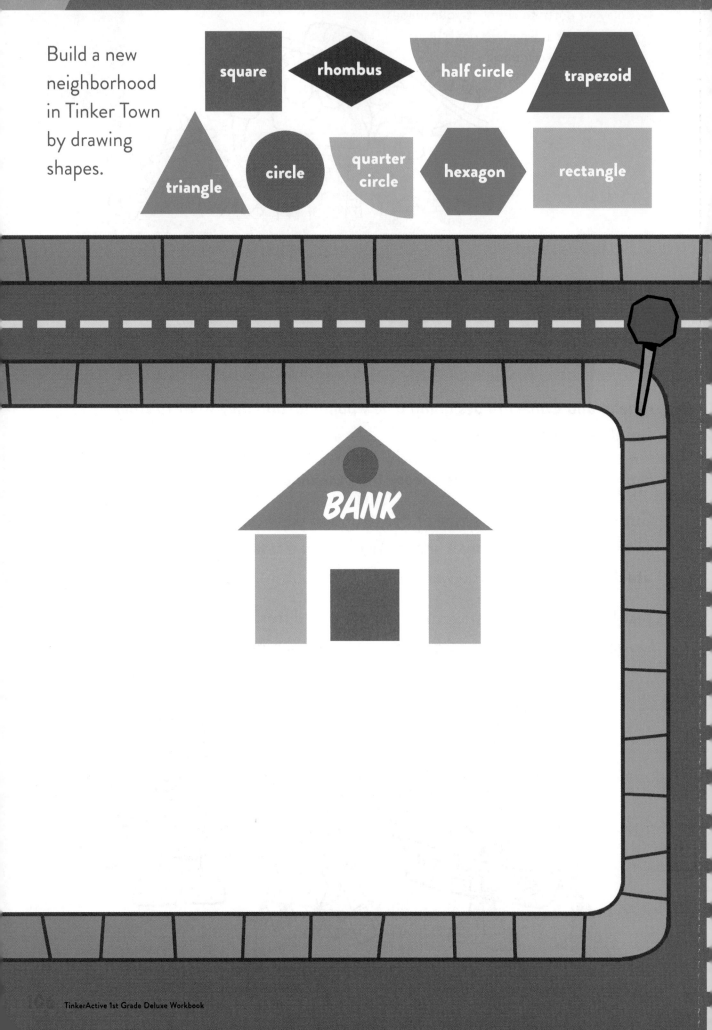

square

rhombus

half circle

trapezoid

triangle

circle

quarter circle

hexagon

rectangle

BANK

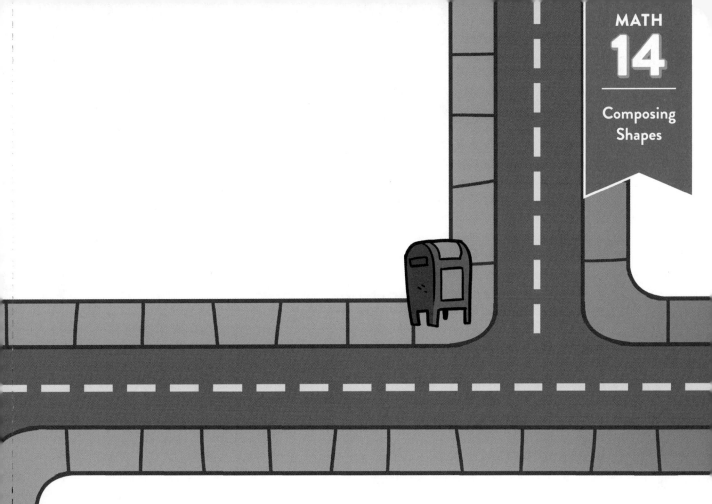

Show your neighborhood
to someone else. Tell them
what shapes you used to
create everything.

Follow the directions.

Draw 2 squares to make a rectangle.

Draw 2 rectangles to make a square.

Draw 4 squares to make a square.

Draw 2 half circles to make a circle.

Draw 2 quarter circles to make a half circle.

Draw 4 quarter circles to make a circle.

Draw 2 triangles to make a rhombus.

Draw 3 triangles to make a trapezoid.

Draw 6 triangles to make a hexagon.

Draw 1 hexagon and 3 triangles to make a large triangle.

How many shapes were put together to make these larger shapes? Color each individual shape with a different color, and then count.

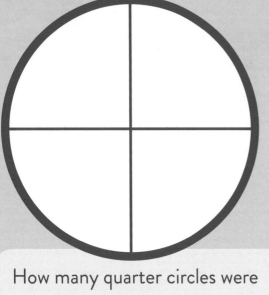

How many triangles were put together to make this trapezoid?

_____

How many quarter circles were put together to make this circle?

_____

How many squares were put together to make this square?

_____

How many squares were put together to make this rectangle?

_____

Draw buildings in Tinker Town using the shapes below.

circular cylinder

rectangular prism

cube

circular cone

Which shape did you use the most? Why?

LET'S START!

GATHER THESE TOOLS AND MATERIALS.

Scissors
(with an adult's help)

Colored pencils, markers,
or crayons

Paper

Cardboard boxes, empty
tissue boxes, or blocks

Toilet paper and paper towel rolls

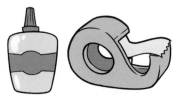

Glue or tape

LET'S TINKER!

Cut out the shapes below and put them together in different combinations. **Make** new shapes or a picture using your shapes.

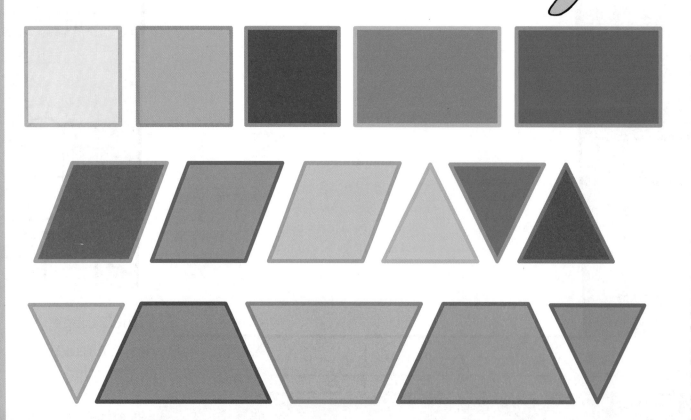

1. **Draw** your dream playhouse.

2. What 3-dimensional shapes will you need for your house? **Gather** the shapes you will need.

3. **Start** building!

LET'S ENGINEER!

The MotMots built their playhouses all over town. Enid built her playhouse in the forest. Frank built his on the beach. Brian built his playhouse on an island, but he wants his friends to come over and play.

How can Brian get his friends across the water to his playhouse?

Build a bridge using different shapes. Which shapes are strongest? How will the bridge stay above water?

Connect your bridge to the playhouse you made.

PROJECT 14: DONE!
Get your sticker!

Dividing Shapes

Draw a line to divide each shape in half.

Is there another way to divide the shapes in half? If so, draw lines using another colored pencil, marker, or crayon.

Circle the shapes in Callie's basket that are divided into equal parts.

Draw two lines to divide each shape into quarters.

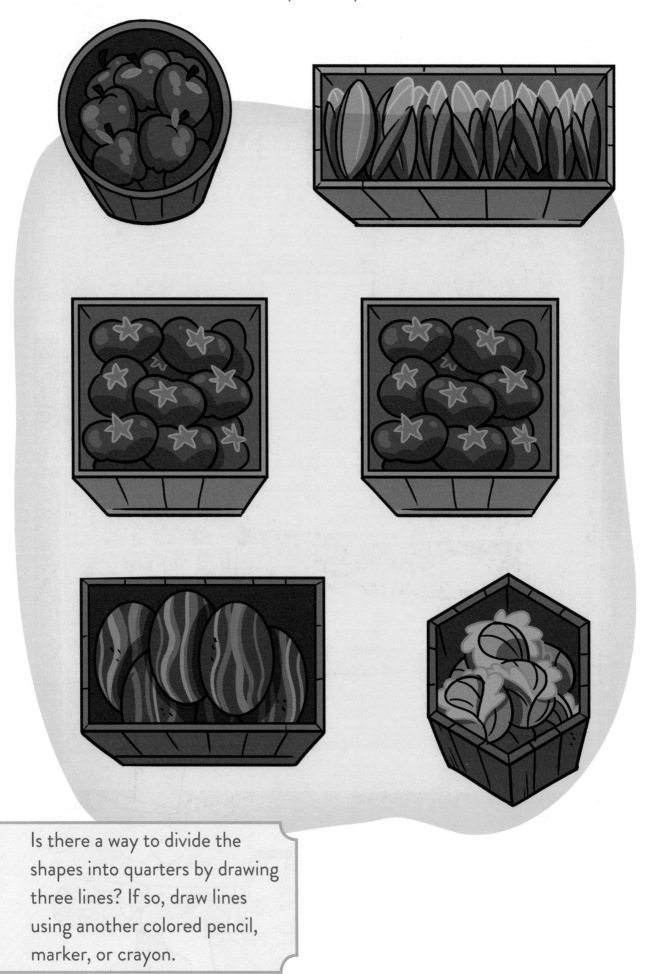

Is there a way to divide the shapes into quarters by drawing three lines? If so, draw lines using another colored pencil, marker, or crayon.

Write whether the shaded part of each shape is a half or a quarter.

_____   _____

_____

_____

_____

Color each shape to make 2 equal parts. Describe the parts aloud, and write whether they are a half or a quarter of the original shape.

Color each shape to make 4 equal parts. Describe the parts aloud, and write whether they are a half or a quarter of the original shape.

LET'S START!

Scissors
(with an adult's help)

Colored pencils, markers,
or crayons

Construction paper

Glue

LET'S TINKER!

There are 3 cakes left at the farmers' market. **Cut** out the cakes below. **Fold** them so that you make pieces that are the same size. If you want to share each cake with a friend, should you divide the cake into halves or quarters?

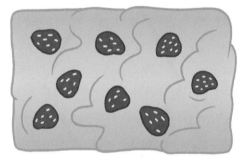

LET'S MAKE: SHAPE SELF-PORTRAIT

1. Cut out the shapes below.

2. Cut each new shape into equal parts.

3. Arrange and glue the parts to create a self-portrait.

LET'S ENGINEER!

The MotMots' favorite spot at the farmers' market is the pizza stand. You get to create your own pizza there! The MotMots want to make a pizza they can share—and they want to make sure everyone gets the same-size slice and the same amount of toppings.

If they need 6 slices, how can the MotMots arrange the toppings so everyone gets the same amount?

Draw a large circle as your pizza. How can you show where to slice the pizza so there are 6 equal pieces? Then **get** sticker toppings from page 385. How can you arrange the toppings so everyone gets the same amount?

PROJECT 15: DONE!
Get your sticker!

ANSWER KEY

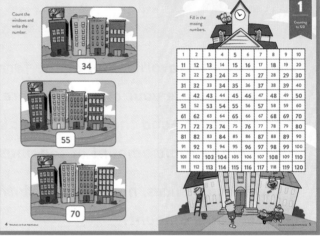

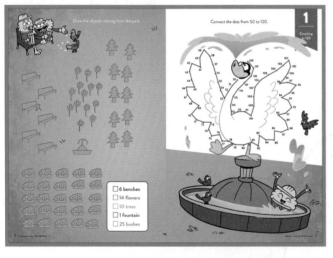

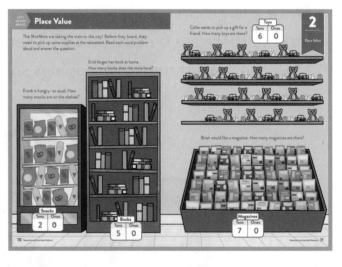

Page 38

Solve each word problem by using the number line. Then write the number sentence.

7 squirrels are running around the park. 2 are red. The others are gray. How many squirrels are gray? — $7 - 2 = 5$

10 fish poke their heads out of the pond. 4 jump back into the water. How many fish are left poking their heads out of the pond? — $10 - 4 = 6$

5 birds are sitting in trees. 10 birds are flying overhead. How many birds are in the park? — $5 + 10 = 15$

13 flowers were under the tree. Some of them were plucked. Now there are 4. How many flowers were plucked? — $13 - 4 = 9$

Page 39 — 5 Word Problems

Dimitri has $12 to spend at the boathouse. Answer each question.

Dimitri wants to rent a fishing rod, a toy ship, and a paddleboat. How much money does he need to rent all 3 items? — $3+5+7=\$15$

Does he have enough money? — No

If not, how much more money does Dimitri need? — $15-12=\$3$

Can he rent more than 1 toy ship? — Yes

Can Dimitri rent more than 1 paddleboat? — No

Can he rent more than 1 fishing rod? — Yes

How many fishing rods, toy ships, or paddleboats would you rent with $12? Write the item or items. — Answers will vary.

Page 42 — Addition & Subtraction Equations

You are a food critic! Circle the thumbs-up next to the equations that are true and the thumbs-down next to the equations that are false.

- $6 - 4 = 3$ 👎
- $8 = 6 + 2$ 👍
- $7 + 3 = 10$ 👍
- $5 + 2 = 7$ 👍
- $8 - 3 = 5$ 👍
- $12 = 6 + 6$ 👍
- $9 + 5 = 14$ 👍
- $7 = 10 - 4$ 👎

Page 43 — 6 Addition & Subtraction Equations

- $11 + 3 = 3 + 11$ 👍
- $6 - 3 = 3 + 6$ 👎
- $3 + 4 = 3 + 5$ 👎
- $5 + 4 = 4 + 5$ 👍

Fix each false number sentence. Fill in the blanks to write a new true number sentence below.

$6 + 4 \neq 2$
$6 + 4 = 10$
$4 + 6 = 10$
$10 - 6 = 4$
$10 - 4 = 6$

$7 \neq 11 - 3$
$8 = 11 - 3$
$3 = 11 - 8$
$8 + 3 = 11$
$3 + 8 = 11$

$12 - 3 \neq 8$
$12 - 4 = 8$
$12 - 8 = 4$
$8 + 4 = 12$
$4 + 8 = 12$

Page 44

Use the numbers at the top of each menu to fill in the blanks. Say each number sentence aloud as you fill it in.

4, 9, 5
$4 + 5 = 9$
$9 - 5 = 4$
$5 + 4 = 9$
$9 - 4 = 5$

2, 10, 8
$2 + 8 = 10$
$10 - 8 = 2$
$8 + 2 = 10$
$10 - 2 = 8$

3, 4, 7
$3 + 4 = 7$
$7 - 4 = 3$
$4 + 3 = 7$
$7 - 3 = 4$

Page 45 — 6 Addition & Subtraction Equations

Amelia must figure out which containers don't have an equal amount of ingredients and refill them. Cross out the containers that are not equal.

- $6 + 5 = 6 + 4$ (crossed out)
- $2 + 9 = 9 + 2$
- $3 + ? = ? + 1$ (crossed out)
- $4 + 8 = 8 + 4$

Page 46

Fill in the missing number to keep the trays balanced.

- 3
- 3
- 8
- 4
- 10

Page 47 — 6 Addition & Subtraction Equations

- 1
- 8
- 6
- 4
- 4

Page 50 — Determining Unknown Numbers

Fill in the missing number on each poster.

WANTED
- $8 - 3 = 5$
- $10 = 15 - 5$
- $14 - 7 = 7$
- $3 + 9 = 12$
- $18 = 13 + 5$
- $3 + 7 = 10$
- $9 + 7 = 16$
- $12 + 8 = 20$
- $6 = 10 - 4$
- $9 - 6 = 3$

Page 52-53 — 7 Determining Unknown Numbers

It's Giving Day in Tinker Town! The MotMots are giving and receiving gifts all day. Read each word problem and fill in the blanks.

Callie had 12 flowers. Now she has 5. Callie gave away 7 flowers!

Brian had 10 crayons. Now he has 5. Brian gave away 5 crayons!

Frank had 9 cookies. Now he has 12. Frank was given 3 more cookies.

Dimitri had 7 balloons. Now he has 11. Dimitri was given 4 more balloons!

Enid had 8 stuffed animals. Now she has 14. Enid was given 6 stuffed animals!

Amelia had 12 baseball cards. Now she has 10. Amelia gave away 2 baseball cards!

Page 54

It's snack time for the dogs. Help feed them by following the instructions.

Sparky has 4 bones and should get 8 bones in total. Draw more bones for Sparky. How many bones did you draw? — 4

Rex has 10 bones. He should have 6. Cross out the number of bones Rex shouldn't have. How many bones did you cross out? — 4

Frenchie has 7 bones. She should have only 3. Cross out the number of bones Frenchie shouldn't have. How many bones did you cross out? — 4

Rosie has 2 bones. She should have 12 in all. Draw more bones for Rosie. How many bones did you draw? — 10

Page 55 — 7 Determining Unknown Numbers

Write the missing number in the number bond. Then fill in the number sentences.

5 (3, 2)
$3 + 2 = 5$
$5 - 2 = 3$
$2 + 3 = 5$
$5 - 3 = 2$

9 (5, 4)
$5 + 4 = 9$
$9 - 4 = 5$
$4 + 5 = 9$
$9 - 5 = 4$

10 (6, 4)
$6 + 4 = 10$
$10 - 6 = 4$
$4 + 6 = 10$
$10 - 4 = 6$

12 (7, 5)
$7 + 5 = 12$
$12 - 7 = 5$
$5 + 7 = 12$
$12 - 5 = 7$

Page 58 — Place Value & Addition

Write the number that is 10 less and the number that is 10 more.

- 15 25 35
- 53 63 73
- 37 47 57
- 9 19 29
- 21 31 41
- 80 90 100

Page 59 — 8 Place Value & Addition

Follow the directions.

Circle the number that is 10 less than 46.

Circle the number that is 10 less than 53.

Circle the number that is 10 more than 17.

Circle the number that is 10 more than 89.

Each display case has bundles of 10 fossils as well as single fossils.
Write the total number of items in each display case.

Place Value & Addition

45

54

67

32

Place Value & Addition

Add to get the letters. Then decode the message on the sarcophagus.

I
40 + 8 = 48

S
20 + 10 = 30

J
30 + 6 = 36

N
5 + 90 = 95

U
1 + 30 = 31

A
80 + 4 = 84

G
70 + 2 = 72

P
50 + 7 = 57

M
90 + 7 = 97

T
10 + 30 = 40

48 84 97   36 31 30 40   95 84 57 57 48 95 72
I A M   J U S T   N A P P I N G

Place Value & Subtraction

Look at the hundreds chart. Then trace the multiples of 10 while reading them aloud.

1	2	3	4	5	6	7	8	9	10
11	12	13	14	15	16	17	18	19	20
21	22	23	24	25	26	27	28	29	30
31	32	33	34	35	36	37	38	39	40
41	42	43	44	45	46	47	48	49	50
51	52	53	54	55	56	57	58	59	60
61	62	63	64	65	66	67	68	69	70
71	72	73	74	75	76	77	78	79	80
81	82	83	84	85	86	87	88	89	90
91	92	93	94	95	96	97	98	99	100

Fill in the missing numbers. Use the hundreds chart to guide you.

Place Value & Subtraction

60 – 40 = 20

30 – 10 = 20

50 – 40 = 10

70 – 20 = 50

90 – 60 = 30

80 – 30 = 50

Place Value & Subtraction

Connect the stars from 100 to zero.
Circle each multiple of 10 as you go!

Place Value & Subtraction

Use the number line to show the difference.

90 – 10 = 80

50 – 40 = 10

20 – 10 = 10

70 – 60 = 10

60 – 10 = 50

90 – 40 = 50

70 – 20 = 50

70 – 30 = 40

50 – 30 = 20

80 – 20 = 60

Measuring & Comparing Lengths

Color the tallest MotMot in each row green. Color the shortest MotMot in each row red. Color the midsize MotMot blue.

Measuring & Comparing Lengths

Color the tallest building in each row green. Color the shortest building in each row red. Color the midsize building blue.

Measuring & Comparing Lengths

Line up paper clips to measure each length and answer each question.

Brian

Who is shorter, Dimitri or Brian?
Brian

Who has the longer leg, Brian or Amelia?
Brian

Who has the shorter arm, Brian or Callie?
Callie

Who has the longer arm, Callie or Dimitri?
Dimitri

Callie

Dimitri

Amelia

Measuring & Comparing Lengths

Choose one of the materials below and circle it. Then, get the object and use it to measure each illustrated object on page 79. Last, record your measurement on the chart.

sugar cubes
toothpicks
paper clips
beans

Object	Measurement
Pencil	Answers will vary.
Spoon	Answers will vary.
Cup	Answers will vary.
Sock	Answers will vary.

List the items from longest to shortest.

1. Sock
2. Pencil
3. Spoon
4. Cup

Do you have any of these objects in your home? Try measuring them!

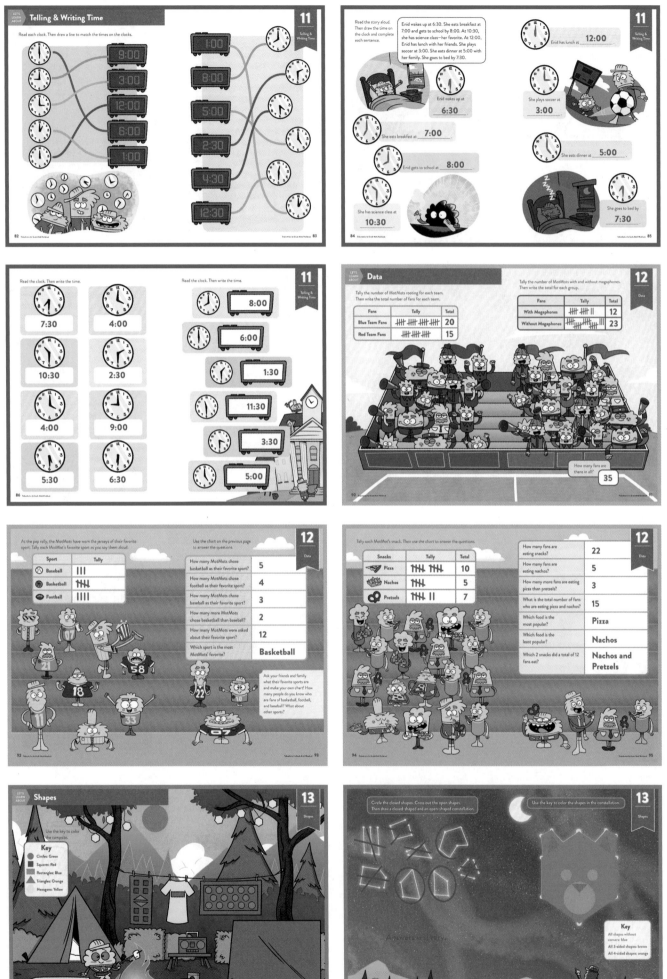

Page 82-83: Telling & Writing Time — Chapter 11

Read each clock. Then draw a line to match the times on the clocks.

9:00
3:00
12:00
6:00
1:00

1:00
8:00
5:00
2:30
4:30
12:30

Page 84-85: Chapter 11 — Telling & Writing Time

Read the story aloud. Then draw the time on the clock and complete each sentence.

Enid wakes up at 6:30. She eats breakfast at 7:00 and gets to school at 8:00. At 10:30, she has science class—her favorite. At 12:00, Enid has lunch with her friends. She plays soccer at 3:00. She eats dinner at 5:00 with her family. She goes to bed by 7:30.

Enid wakes up at **6:30**
She eats breakfast at **7:00**
Enid gets to school at **8:00**
She has science class at **10:30**
Enid has lunch at **12:00**
She plays soccer at **3:00**
She eats dinner at **5:00**
She goes to bed by **7:30**

Page 86: Chapter 11 — Telling & Writing Time

Read the clock. Then write the time.

7:30 | 4:00
10:30 | 2:30
4:00 | 9:00
5:30 | 6:30

Read the clock. Then write the time.

8:00
6:00
1:30
11:30
3:30
5:00

Page 90-91: Data — Chapter 12

Tally the number of MotMots rooting for each team. Then write the total number of fans for each team.

Fans	Tally	Total
Blue Team Fans	✝✝✝ ✝✝✝ ✝✝✝ ✝✝✝	20
Red Team Fans	✝✝✝ ✝✝✝ ✝✝✝	15

Tally the number of MotMots with and without megaphones. Then write the total for each group.

Fans	Tally	Total
With Megaphones	✝✝✝ ✝✝✝ ✝✝	12
Without Megaphones	✝✝✝ ✝✝✝ ✝✝✝ ✝✝✝ ✝✝✝	23

How many fans are there in all? **35**

Page 92-93: Chapter 12

At the pep rally, the MotMots have worn the jerseys of their favorite sport. Tally each MotMot's favorite sport as you say them aloud.

Sport	Tally
Baseball	III
Basketball	✝✝✝
Football	IIII

Use the chart on the previous page to answer the questions.

How many MotMots chose basketball as their favorite sport?	5
How many MotMots chose football as their favorite sport?	4
How many MotMots chose baseball as their favorite sport?	3
How many more MotMots chose basketball than baseball?	2
How many MotMots were asked about their favorite sport?	12
Which sport is the most MotMots' favorite?	Basketball

Ask your friends and family what their favorite sports are and make your own chart! How many people do you know who are fans of basketball, football, and baseball? What about other sports?

Page 94-95: Chapter 12

Tally each MotMot's snack. Then use the chart to answer the questions.

Snacks	Tally	Total
Pizza	✝✝✝ ✝✝✝	10
Nachos	✝✝✝	5
Pretzels	✝✝✝ II	7

How many fans are eating snacks?	22
How many fans are eating nachos?	5
How many more fans are eating pizza than pretzels?	3
What is the total number of fans who are eating pizza and nachos?	15
Which food is the most popular?	Pizza
Which food is the least popular?	Nachos
Which 2 snacks did a total of 12 fans eat?	Nachos and Pretzels

Page 100-101: Shapes — Chapter 13

Use the key to color the campsite.

Key
- Circles: Green
- Square: Red
- Rectangles: Blue
- Triangles: Orange
- Hexagons: Yellow

Circle the closed shapes. Cross out the open shapes. Then draw a closed-shaped and an open-shaped constellation.

Use the key to color the shapes in the constellation.

Key
All shapes without corners: blue
All 3-sided shapes: brown
All 4-sided shapes: orange

Answers will vary.

Page 13 — Shapes

Read the text aloud. Then draw the shape and write the name.

- I have zero straight sides and zero corners. What shape am I? — **circle**
- I have 3 straight sides and 3 corners. What shape am I? — **triangle**
- I have 4 straight sides and 4 corners. What shape am I? — **square** or **rectangle**
- I have 6 straight sides and 6 corners. What shape am I? — **hexagon**

Read about 3-dimensional shapes.

- All rectangular prisms have 6 faces.
- All cylinders are solid shapes.
- All spheres are round.
- All pyramids are made of triangles.

Then fill in the blanks in the story with words from the box.

curved   triangles   rectangular prism
sphere   cylinder   pyramid   six

The MotMots went camping for Enid's birthday! Enid brought a book to read by the campfire. The book was a **rectangular prism** and had **six** faces. For lunch, Frank packed his favorite—a giant can of tomato soup. The can was a **cylinder**—just like the mugs they used to drink it. After lunch, the MotMots played baseball. The baseball bat was a cylinder, but the baseball was a **sphere**. The sides of the baseball and baseball bat were **curved**. Amelia hit a home run! At night, the MotMots slept in a tent. It was in the shape of a **pyramid**. The sides of their tent were shaped like **triangles**. Before they went to bed, they watched the sky. The moon looked like half a sphere, and Enid even saw a shooting star. Enid had a very happy birthday!

102 / 103

Page 14 — Composing Shapes

Build a new neighborhood in Tinker Town by drawing shapes.

square   rhombus   half circle   trapezoid
triangle   circle   quarter circle   hexagon   rectangle

Answers will vary.

BANK

Answers will vary.

Answers will vary.

Show your neighborhood to someone else. Tell them what shapes you used to create everything.

Page 14 (continued) — Composing Shapes

Follow the directions.

- Draw 2 squares to make a rectangle. — Answers will vary.
- Draw 2 rectangles to make a square. — Answers will vary.
- Draw 4 quarter circles to make a circle. — Answers will vary.
- Draw 2 triangles to make a rhombus. — Answers will vary.
- Draw 4 squares to make a square. — Answers will vary.
- Draw 2 half circles to make a circle. — Answers will vary.
- Draw 3 triangles to make a trapezoid. — Answers will vary.
- Draw 2 quarter circles to make a half circle. — Answers will vary.
- Draw 6 triangles to make a hexagon. — Answers will vary.
- Draw 3 hexagon and 3 triangles to make a large triangle. — Answers will vary.

108 / 109

Page 14 (continued)

How many shapes were put together to make these larger shapes? Color each individual shape with a different color, and then count.

- How many quarter circles were put together to make this circle? **4**
- How many triangles were put together to make this trapezoid? **8**
- How many squares were put together to make this square? **16**
- How many squares were put together to make this rectangle? **24**

Draw buildings in Tinker Town using the shapes below.

circular cylinder   rectangular prism   cube   circular cone

Answers will vary.

Which shape did you use the most? Why?

110

Page 15 — Dividing Shapes

Draw a line to divide each shape in half. **Answers will vary.**

Circle the shapes in Callie's basket that are divided into equal parts.

Is there another way to divide the shapes in half? If so, draw lines using another colored pencil, marker, or crayon. Answers will vary.

114 / 115

Page 15 (continued)

Draw two lines to divide each shape into quarters. **Answers will vary.**

Write whether the shaded part of each shape is a half or a quarter.

Quarter   Half   Quarter   Half   Half   Quarter   Half

FARM FRESH 25¢

Is there a way to divide the shapes into quarters by drawing three lines? If so, draw lines using another colored pencil, marker, or crayon. Answers will vary.

116 / 117

Page 15 (continued)

Color each shape to make 2 equal parts. Describe the parts aloud, and write whether they are a half or a quarter of the original shape.

Half   Half   Half   Half   Half   Half

FARM FRESH 25¢

Color each shape to make 4 equal parts. Describe the parts aloud, and write whether they are a half or a quarter of the original shape.

Quarter   Quarter   Quarter   Quarter   Quarter   Quarter

118 / 119

1ST GRADE · SCIENCE · AGES 6–7

by Megan Hewes Butler

illustrated by Lauren Pettapiece and Les McClaine

educational consulting by Amanda Raupe

 Odd Dot · New York

Earth

Earth is the planet we live on. It is made of rock and surrounded by air. There is land and water. Color the land green. Color the water blue.

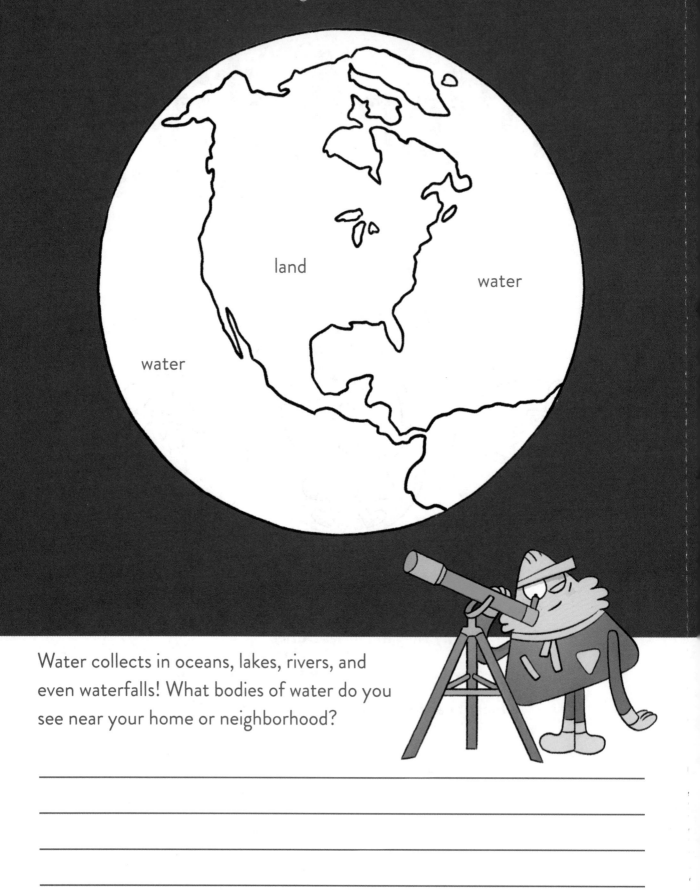

land

water

water

Water collects in oceans, lakes, rivers, and even waterfalls! What bodies of water do you see near your home or neighborhood?

_____

_____

_____

_____

Earth's surface has the air, water, and dirt that plants, animals, and people need to live. Circle the living things. Then draw yourself on Earth's surface.

Look around your home. What living things do you see?

_____

_____

_____

_____

_____

Read the text aloud. Then circle the correct label for each picture.

Earth is always spinning. Some parts spin to face the Sun and some parts spin away. The part of Earth facing the Sun has light and it is daytime. The part of Earth facing away from the Sun has darkness and it is nighttime.

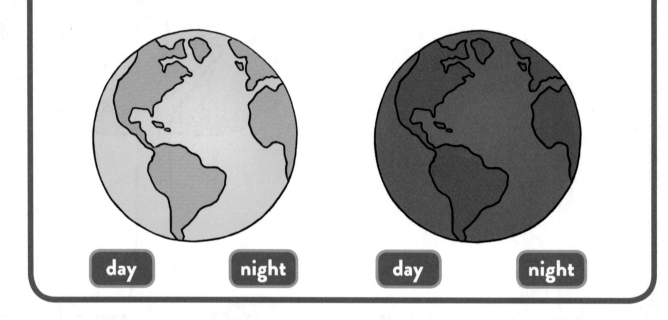

day   **night**   **day**   **night**

Each day the Sun appears to rise as Earth spins. During the day, we see it travel across the sky. Each night the Sun appears to set. Earth spins and we can no longer see the Sun until the next morning.

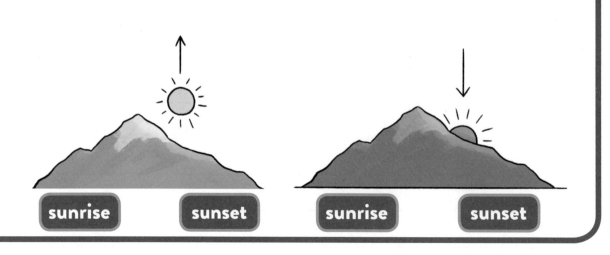

sunrise   **sunset**   **sunrise**   **sunset**

Draw lines to connect each activity to the time of day it usually occurs.

day

night

Earth travels around the Sun once per year. The path it moves on is called its orbit. The way the Sun's rays hit Earth as it orbits gives us seasons.

Direct, strong rays cause hotter temperatures in the summer, when days are longer.

Less direct, weaker rays cause colder temperatures in the winter, when days are shorter.

Different locations on Earth have their seasons at different times based on the tilt of Earth toward or away from the Sun. Seasons repeat at the same times every year. It takes 365 days for Earth to orbit the Sun one time.

Circle the correct words in each sentence.

In the summer, the days are **long** / **short**.

In the winter, the days are **long** / **short**.

The seasons happen at **the same time** / **different times** every year.

Every year, the seasons repeat: summer, fall, winter, and spring.

Look out your window. What season is it now? Write about or draw how you know what season it is.

How do you dress for this season? Draw the clothes you wear.

What season is coming next where you live?

_____

LET'S START! GATHER THESE TOOLS AND MATERIALS.

5 or more rocks

4–6 leaves

4–6 sticks

Trowel

Paper plate

4–6 toothpicks

Shoebox

LET'S TINKER!

There are many patterns on Earth, like day and night, sunrise and sunset, and the seasons.

Create patterns with your materials. Which materials can you repeat? Can you make short patterns? Can you make long patterns?

LET'S MAKE: SUNDIAL!

Earth is always spinning, so the Sun's rays hit it differently throughout the day. **Make** a sundial, which is a simple device for telling time by watching shadows move as Earth spins!

1. On a sunny day, **dig** a small hole in the dirt and **place** one end of a stick in the ground, pointing straight up.

2. Use one of your objects, like a rock, to mark where the stick's shadow is on the ground.

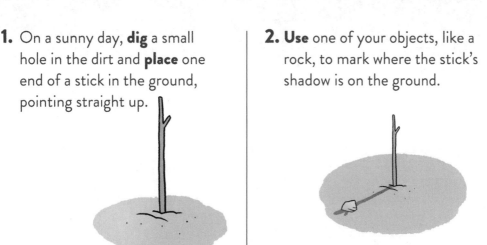

3. Predict where you think the shadow will be in 10 minutes, 1 hour, much later in the day, and tomorrow morning. **Use** other objects to mark where you think the shadow will move to.

4. Check your sundial at different points in the day. Were your predictions correct? Did you observe any patterns? Where did the shadow move to?

LET'S ENGINEER!

Frank's class is getting an insect as a new pet! But it's a surprise— no one knows exactly what kind of insect it will be. How can Frank provide his new pet with everything it needs to survive when he doesn't know what kind it is?

Set up a habitat with things an insect would need to survive. Use your shoebox as a home. Which materials can be used to make a shelter? Can any of your materials work as food? Where can you put the water?

Look for other materials around your home that can help.

PROJECT 1: DONE!
Get your sticker!

Solar System

Earth is a planet in our solar system. Our solar system is made up of the Sun, eight planets and their moons, and other, smaller objects like asteroids, meteoroids, and comets.

Sun

Circle Earth. How do you know it's Earth?

_____

Using the stickers on page 387, show the Moon orbiting Earth. Draw arrows to show how Earth is spinning.

What is at the center of our solar system? _____. Put the correct sticker from page 387 on it.

asteroid

planets

Draw an X on the largest object in our solar system.

comet

Earth is the only planet with one moon. Jupiter and Saturn each have over fifty moons!

Earth is one of the eight planets that orbit our Sun. Each of these planets is unique. Here are the planets in order from closest to the Sun to farthest from the Sun.

Mercury—the closest planet to the Sun. Mercury is also the smallest planet in our solar system.

Venus—the brightest planet in the sky. Venus's thick clouds reflect lots of light. You can sometimes see Venus from Earth during the day!

Earth—the only planet known to have life on it: plants, animals, and people. We live on Earth!

Mars—a rusty red planet. Iron on Mars's surface rusts, giving the planet its color.

Jupiter—the largest planet in our solar system. Jupiter is over 300 times larger than Earth!

Saturn—the planet with the most rings. Saturn has seven ring groups, each of which is made up of thousands of smaller rings. You can even see them from Earth!

Uranus—the planet tipped over on its side. Uranus spins in such a way that its north and south poles face the Sun as it orbits.

Neptune—the farthest planet from the Sun. It was also the last one to be discovered. It takes 165 Earth years for Neptune to orbit the Sun.

Write the name of each planet in our solar system. Then say the names aloud, from the planet closest to the Sun to the planet farthest from the Sun.

On Earth, we have earthquakes.
But on Mars, there are marsquakes!

Draw a line to match each object to the correct definition.

The **Sun** is the biggest object in our solar system. It is a star—a hot ball of burning gas.

A **planet** is an object in space that moves around a star. Saturn is a planet that orbits the Sun.

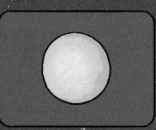

A **comet** is a frozen object made of ice and dust that orbits the Sun. It can have a tail.

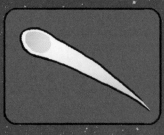

A **moon** is an object in space that orbits a planet.

An **asteroid** is a jagged object made mostly of rock and metal that orbits the Sun.

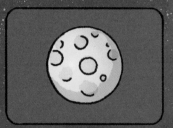

A scientist who studies space is called an astronomer. A telescope is one of the tools an astronomer uses to see objects that are far away in space.

Write about and draw what you'd like to see using a telescope. You can also use stickers from page 387.

_____

_____

LET'S START!

GATHER THESE TOOLS AND MATERIALS.

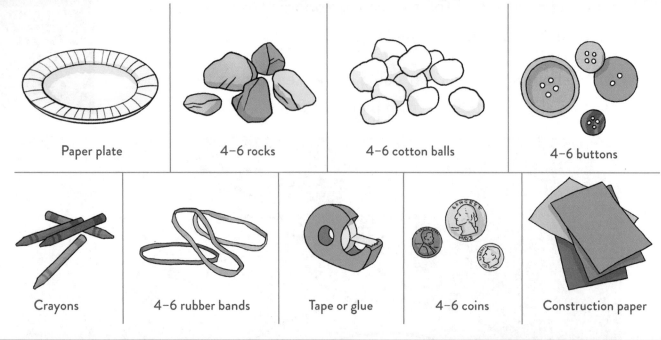

Paper plate	4–6 rocks	4–6 cotton balls	4–6 buttons
Crayons	4–6 rubber bands	Tape or glue	4–6 coins	Construction paper

LET'S TINKER!

Our solar system is filled with objects that are on the move. Comets and asteroids are flying through space. All the planets, including Earth, are spinning as they orbit the Sun.

Spin your materials. Can any of them spin around or fly? What happens if they run into one another?

LET'S MAKE: YOUR OWN PLANET!

Use the materials to make your own made-up planet.

1. Pick a round object, like a paper plate, as the base for your planet.

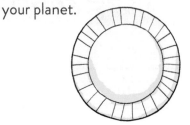

2. Color your planet with crayons.

3. Give your planet rings or craters. **Name** your planet!

LET'S ENGINEER!

Brian is studying the solar system and wants to remember the order of the eight planets. He knows that Mercury comes first, but what comes next?

How can Brian remember all the planets in order?

Make a model of the eight planets in order. **Design** a way to remember their names. Which planets are small and which are large? Can you add the Sun to your model?

PROJECT 2: DONE!
Get your sticker!

Sun, Moon & Stars

There is only one star in our solar system—the Sun. It is a ball of burning gases that provides the light and heat we need to survive on Earth. Even though it is far away, the Sun is so bright that we cannot look directly at it. Its rays are so powerful that we have to protect our skin so it doesn't burn.

Circle the things you use to protect yourself from the Sun's rays.

The Sun is always shining, but we cannot always see it because Earth spins. When the part of Earth that we are on is facing the Sun, it is day. When the part of Earth that we are on rotates away from the Sun, it is night.

Color the side of Earth reached by the Sun's rays yellow. Color the side of Earth that no light is reaching black.

Read the poem aloud.

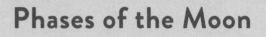

Phases of the Moon

Some planets have many moons
and some have none.
On Earth we are lucky—
we have one!

Our moon circles Earth
on a month-long path.
We call this an orbit—
now comes the math.

The Sun shines upon the Moon
and lights up different places.
Each new look has a name—
we call them the Moon's phases!

A full moon shows its whole face.
A new moon hides its light.
A half-moon is half-shadowed,
while the other half is bright.

The Moon is waxing when it's growing
and waning when it's not.
It's crescent when there's less than half
and gibbous when there's a lot.

The phase of the Moon is always changing,
and now that you know the reasons,
you can watch and track the patterns,
even through the seasons!

Color the phases of the Moon that we see from Earth. Use yellow to color the parts of the Moon lit up by the Sun. Use **black** to color the parts of the Moon we cannot see.

half

gibbous

crescent

full

new

gibbous

crescent

half

Look out your window at night. Can you see the Moon? Which phase is it in?

_____

Stars are balls of burning gases. Groups of stars in a pattern can form a constellation. Connect the dots to form constellations.

Draw what you see outside your window at night. Can you find a constellation? If so, draw it. If not, draw your own pattern of stars.

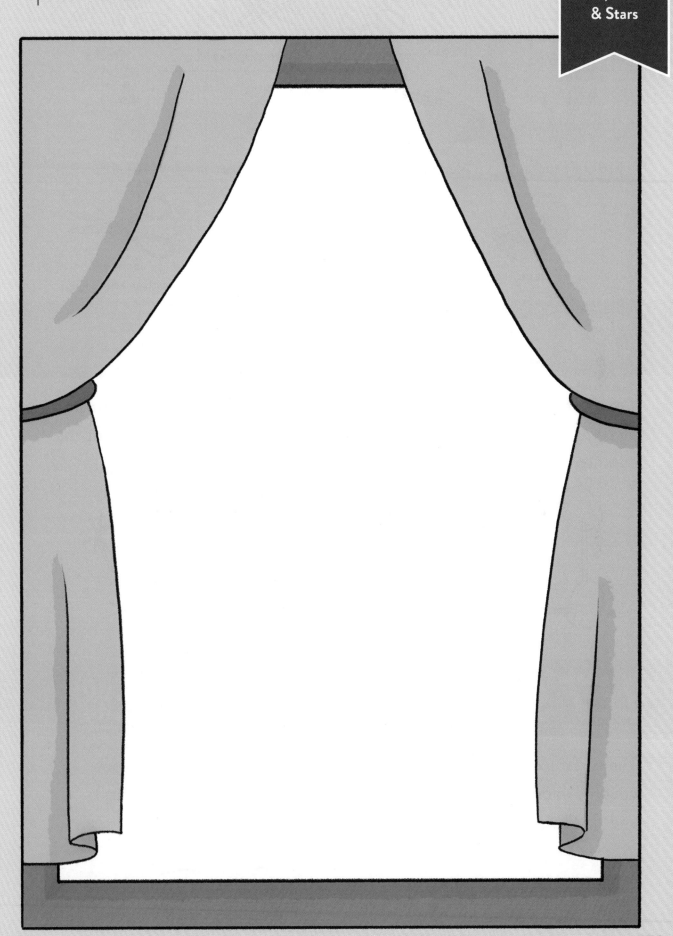

LET'S START!

Piece of string 2–3 feet long

4–6 cotton balls

4–6 toothpicks

Rocks

4–6 craft sticks

Aluminum foil

Construction paper

Glue

Tape

Markers or crayons

Scissors
(with an adult's help)

LET'S TINKER!

Create stars with your materials. Can you combine your stars to form any pictures, like constellations? Which materials can be used to represent the darkness of night?

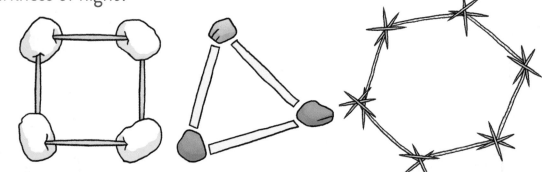

LET'S MAKE: METEORS AND CRATERS!

The surface of the Moon is covered in craters—large and small dents caused by asteroids and meteorites crashing into it.

Find rocks of different sizes and a spot outside with dirt or sand (and no grass) where it is safe to throw rocks.

1. The rocks will be your meteorites—**throw**, **drop**, **toss**, and **fling** them at the ground.

2. Watch what happens when the rocks hit the ground and make craters.

How does the dirt or sand change? That's a crater! Do different rocks make craters that look the same? How can you throw a rock differently to change the size and shape of the craters it makes?

LET'S ENGINEER!

Enid is throwing an ice pop party for her pet spider. She doesn't want the tiny frozen ice pops to melt.

How can Enid keep her ice pops cool on a hot day?

Design something to create shade for the ice pops. How can you use your materials to help? How many spiders and tiny ice pops could fit inside?

PROJECT 3 DONE!
Get your sticker!

Parts of a Plant

Plants have different parts that help them live and grow.

Roots collect water and nutrients, and they hold the plant firmly in the ground.

A **stem** or **trunk** holds the plant or tree up and transports water and nutrients to the leaves, flowers, and fruits.

Leaves collect sunlight and make food for the plant. They also make oxygen.

Flowers grow seeds for the plant.

Fruits provide protection for the seeds. They also help spread the seeds through wind, water, or animals.

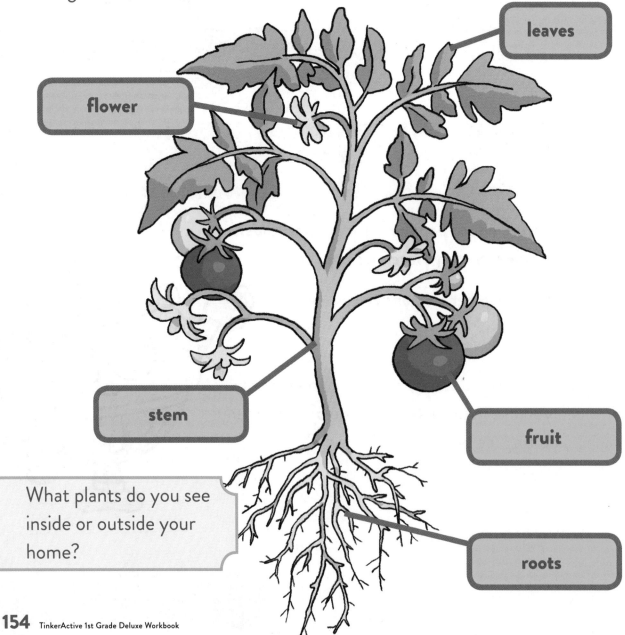

leaves

flower

stem

fruit

roots

What plants do you see inside or outside your home?

Label the parts of the plants in Brian's garden.

Which parts can you
see on the plants
near you?

Plants use their different parts to help them live and grow in different habitats.

Connect each plant to its habitat.

Bearberry plants have dark leaves and low stems. This helps them absorb heat from the Sun and from Earth so they can survive in very cold temperatures.

Agave leaves have a waxy coating to protect the water inside the plant. This helps them survive in hot habitats with little rainfall.

Bromeliads grow on other plants instead of in the ground. This helps them get closer to the Sun when the plants around them are tall.

Water lilies have stems and leaves that can bend and move. This helps them live in underwater habitats.

RAIN FOREST

FRESH WATER

DESERT

TUNDRA

Look at how each plant uses its parts to live and grow. Then design your own solution to each problem.

A peanut shell protects the seeds inside.

Write about and draw a solution you can use to protect your lunch on the way to school.

_____

_____

_____

A tree's branches hold the leaves up high to get light from the Sun.

Write about and draw a solution you can use to hold a wet swimsuit and towel up to the Sun to dry.

LET'S START!

Tape or glue

4–6 twist ties

Aluminum foil

4–6 cotton swabs

Paper towel tube

1 paper towel

4–6 paper cups

Spoon

Scissors
(with an adult's help)

Markers

LET'S TINKER!

Play with your materials to create pictures or sculptures of plant parts. Can you **make** seeds, fruits, leaves, flowers, roots, and a stem or trunk?

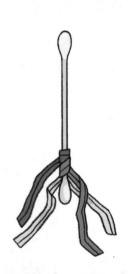

LET'S MAKE: RAINBOW ROOTS!

1. Fill a cup halfway with water.

2. Take a paper towel and **cut** off a narrow strip.

3. Draw a rainbow on the paper towel strip with markers.

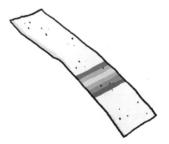

4. Fold the paper towel strip in half and **place** it over a spoon balanced on top of the cup. The ends of the paper towel should dip into the water.

5. Watch what happens. How does the paper towel change? Feel the paper towel—what do you notice? What happens to the water in the cup?

LET'S ENGINEER!

Dimitri is constructing a toy castle and he wants to add a tower. But Dimitri's tower keeps falling over! He knows that the stem and trunk hold a plant up, and the roots hold it firmly in the ground.

How can he build a tower that won't fall over?

Design a tower that stands strong and tall, just like some plants do. Which materials can help you build it taller? Which can help you build it stronger?

Try putting your tower on a table and then shaking the table. Is your tower still standing? If not, build it stronger.

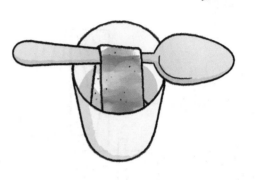

PROJECT 4 DONE!
Get your sticker!

Plant Growth

Plants are living things. They need light, air, water, and nutrients from the dirt to live and grow. Help Dimitri water his plants with the watering can. Draw a line through the maze to visit each plant.

What are other ways that plants can get the water they need to survive?

_____

_____

Plants all need the same things to live, whether they are growing indoors or outdoors. Color each plant's light source **yellow**. Color each plant's water source blue. Color each plant's nutrient source brown.

Plants respond to changes in their environment to keep getting the things they need to live and grow. Draw how each plant changes to meet its needs.

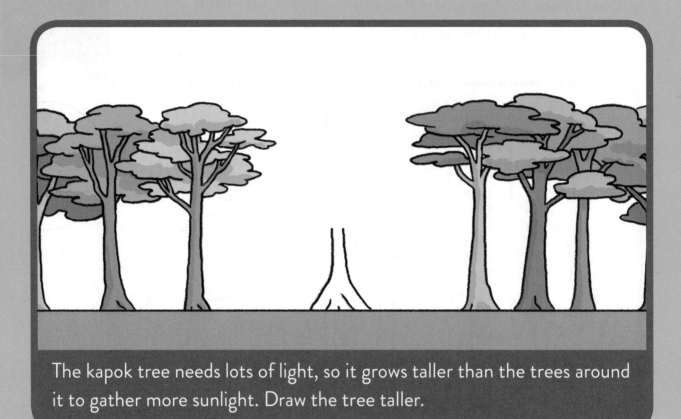

The kapok tree needs lots of light, so it grows taller than the trees around it to gather more sunlight. Draw the tree taller.

The tulip plant needs its pollen to make seeds, so it closes its petals to protect its pollen when it rains. Draw a tulip plant closed.

The spruce tree needs water. During a drought, when there is very little rain, the roots grow deeper to find the water the tree needs.
Draw the roots deeper.

This indoor fern needs sunlight, so it grows toward the window to get more light. Draw the fern's leaves growing closer to the window.

Plants change as they grow, but they continue to look similar to their parent. These leaves blew away in the wind. Observe and compare them to the trees. Draw a line to connect each leaf to the type of tree it belonged to.

OAK   BIRCH   MAPLE

Which pairs of leaves come from the same type of tree? Color each pair of leaves the same color.

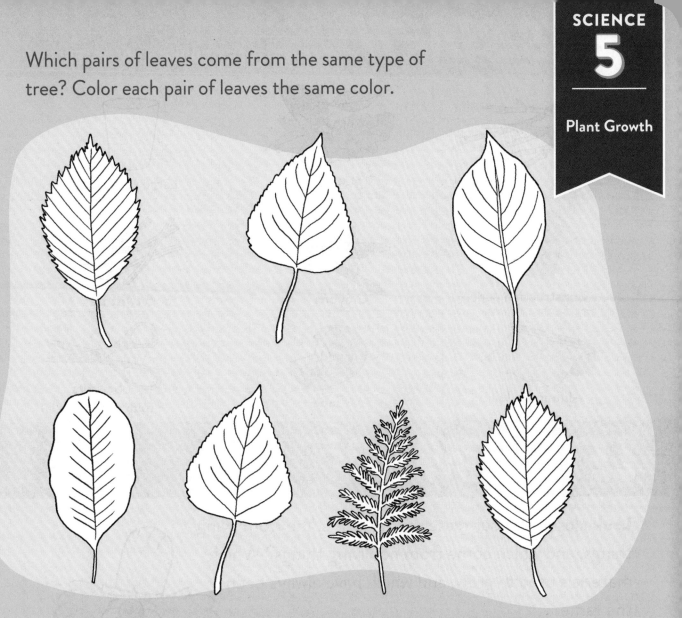

Go on a leaf hunt around your home or neighborhood. Write about or draw the leaves that you find. Do any of your leaves come from the same kinds of trees?

LET'S START!

GATHER THESE TOOLS AND MATERIALS.

3–5 sticks	3–5 leaves	Large paper cup
Construction paper	Crayons	3–5 twist ties
Aluminum foil	Tape	Scissors (with an adult's help)

LET'S TINKER!

Look closely at your materials. Which come from living things, and which come from nonliving things? Which materials used to grow, and which have always been the same?

Break or **tear** pieces off some of your materials. What's on the inside? How are the insides of living things different from the insides of nonliving things?

LET'S MAKE: POLLEN-FILLED FLOWERS!

Some flowers close at night or in the rain to keep their pollen safe and dry. **Make** your own flower that can open to allow insects to reach the pollen and close to keep the pollen safe.

1. **Take** one stick or **tie** a bunch of sticks together with twist ties.

2. Tape leaves to the bottom or **make** your own leaves by cutting them out of construction paper.

3. Tear or **cut** out pieces of the aluminum foil to make flower petals you can bend open and closed. **Tape** them to the top.

4. Create pollen by cutting the construction paper, foil, or leaves into tiny pieces and hiding them inside your petals.

LET'S ENGINEER!

Callie has a few small plants in her cup. They have dirt, air, and water, but Callie's plants keep dying!

How can Callie keep her plants alive?

Use your cup and some leaves to show how you would plant something so it had all it needed to survive. Is Callie's plant missing light, air, water, or dirt? **Test** your solution by a window to see if your plant is getting all four. Is light able to make it to your leaves?

PROJECT 5 DONE!
Get your sticker!

Plant Life Cycle

All plants can produce more young plants. In the plant life cycle below, circle the seed sprouting into a new young plant.

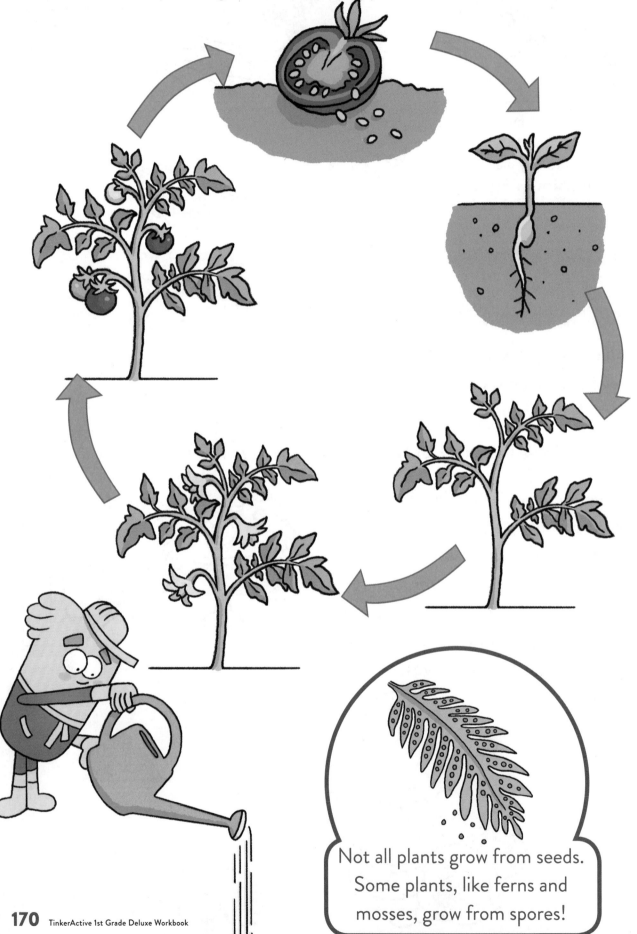

Not all plants grow from seeds. Some plants, like ferns and mosses, grow from spores!

Write the numbers 1, 2, 3, 4, and 5 to put the life cycle of each plant in order from youngest to oldest.

WATERMELON PLANT

PEA PLANT

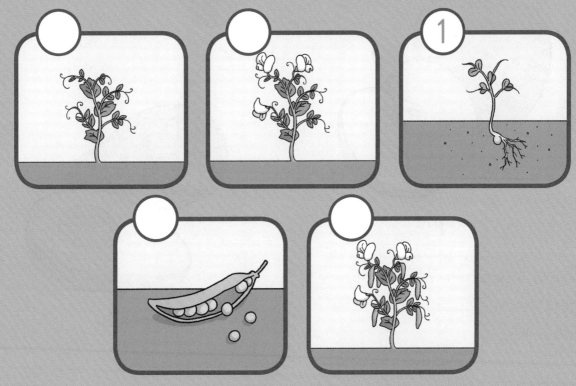

Many plants grow seeds inside their fruits. You can eat the fruits, then plant the seeds.

Circle the seeds inside of each fruit.

peach

kiwi

cantaloupe

cherry

orange

apple

Go to your kitchen. What fruit or vegetable can you bite into to see some seeds?

avocado

Read the poem aloud. Then label the parts of the seed.

Seeds

A seed is the start of a new plant,
with all it needs to survive.
Seeds can be any shape or size—
any color of seed will thrive!

The **seed coat** wraps the seed up tight,
protecting what's inside.
The **endosperm** is just beneath,
holding food for the seed's ride.

The most important part of the seed
we've saved for very last.
The **embryo** is wrapped up safe,
its cells ready to start growing fast.

Seeds travel in different ways. Some travel in the wind. Some travel when animals eat them and carry them to new places.

sunflower

maple

willow

apple

dandelion

rosewood

blackberry

acorn

Look at the seeds on page 174. Then fill in the chart with the seeds that you predict travel in the wind and the seeds that you predict are eaten by animals.

How Do Seeds Move?

In the Wind	Eaten by Animals
rosewood	apple

When you pick a dandelion and blow on it, what happens? Go outside, find another seed, and draw it.

LET'S START!

GATHER THESE TOOLS AND MATERIALS.

4–6 cotton balls

Paper

Crayons or markers

Scissors
(with an adult's help)

Tape

Aluminum foil

4–6 rubber bands

4–6 paper clips

LET'S TINKER!

Many seeds grow inside of fruits, like apples. Other seeds grow on the outside of fruits, like strawberries.

Look at your materials. Which could look like the seeds inside a fruit? Which could look like the seeds outside a fruit? Try to **re-create** both types of seeds.

LET'S MAKE: SPINNING SEEDS!

Seeds move in different ways in the wind. They can float, fly, drop, glide, or even spin. **Make** your own spinning seed like a helicopter!

1. Cut and **fold** the template on page 176 as shown. Cut on the solid lines. Fold on the dashed lines.

2. Use one of your materials, like a rubber band or paper clip, as a weight on the bottom.

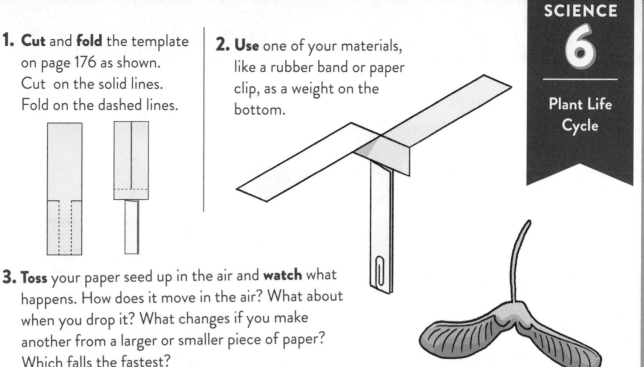

3. Toss your paper seed up in the air and **watch** what happens. How does it move in the air? What about when you drop it? What changes if you make another from a larger or smaller piece of paper? Which falls the fastest?

LET'S ENGINEER!

Frank wants to send a secret note to Dimitri, who is sitting across the room.

How can he get the note to Dimitri quickly and quietly?

Design a solution to move a note through the air like a seed. **Start** with a note written on a large or small piece of paper. How can you fold or cut the paper to help it move? Which other materials can you use to help the message fly, glide, or spin? How far can your note travel?

PROJECT 6 DONE!
Get your sticker!

Types of Animals

There are two types of animals: vertebrates and invertebrates. Vertebrates are animals with backbones, like cows. Invertebrates are animals without backbones, like bees.

Draw a line to match each vertebrate to its description.

I am a mammal who has pointed ears and whiskers.

I am called a "bird of prey" because of my hunting skills. I live high up in a nest made of sticks.

I can move in the water and on land. I don't need to drink water because I absorb it through my skin.

hawk

frog

cat

Draw a line to match each invertebrate to its description.

snail

starfish

spider

I live in water. I have five arms, and if I lose one, I can grow a new one.

I am an arachnid. I make silk and spin webs.

I make a hard shell to live in.

Read about the types of vertebrates. Then draw a line to connect each animal to its type.

Reptiles live on land, breathe air, and lay eggs.

Birds have feathers, beaks, and wings.

Fish live in the water. They have gills and scales.

swordfish

Gila monster

Amphibians live in the water and on land, but they do not have any scales.

Mammals are covered in hair and make milk to feed their young.

poison dart frog

bald eagle

zebra

Two types of invertebrates are insects, like an ant, and arachnids, like a tarantula.

All insects have six legs. They also have three important body parts—a head, a middle section called a thorax, and an abdomen. Many insects also have wings.

Add the missing labels for each insect.

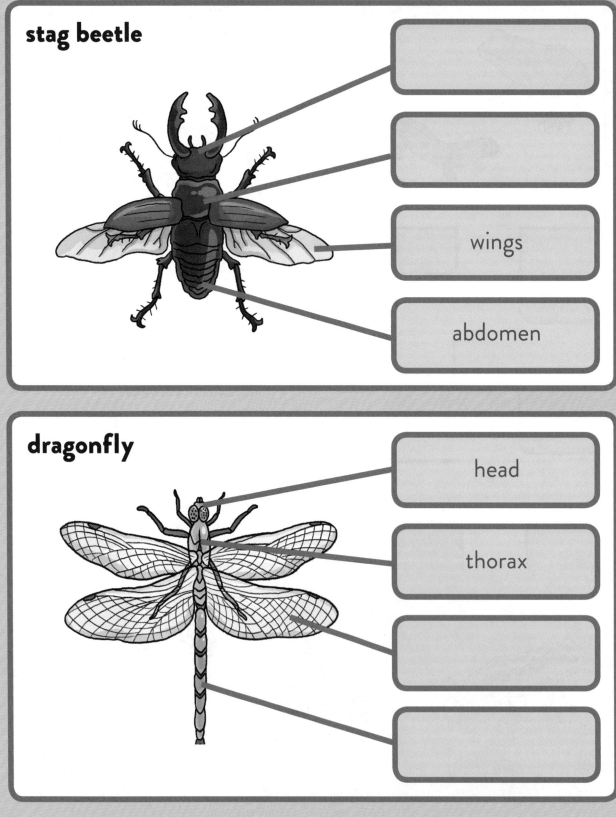

stag beetle

wings

abdomen

dragonfly

head

thorax

All arachnids have eight legs. They also have two main body parts—an abdomen and a combined head and thorax called a cephalothorax.

Count the legs of each invertebrate. Circle the insects. Then put a square around the arachnids.

scorpion

mite

tarantula

fly

grass spider

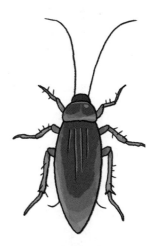

cockroach

mouse spider

grasshopper

LET'S START! GATHER THESE TOOLS AND MATERIALS.

6 or more cotton balls	Tissues	6 or more toothpicks or cotton swabs
Construction paper	Glue / Tape	Paper plate
12 or more pieces of dried pasta	Aluminum foil	Scissors (with an adult's help)

LET'S TINKER!

Animals are classified into two types, vertebrates and invertebrates, by whether or not they have a backbone.

Classify and **sort** your materials. Can they be divided into hard and soft groups? Rigid and bendable? Natural and man-made? Dark and light?

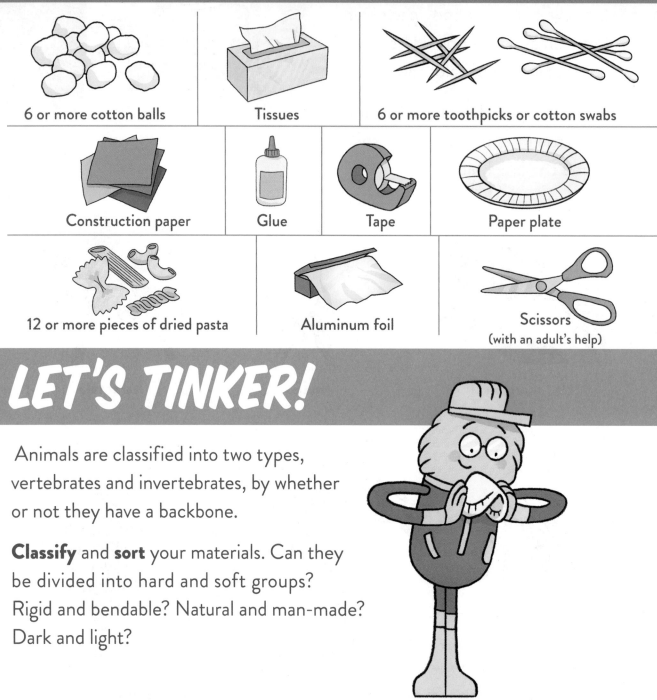

LET'S MAKE: SKELETONS!

A vertebrate has a backbone that shapes its body and protects what's inside. The backbone and the body are covered by skin. **Build** your own backbone or skeleton of a human or an animal.

1. **Use** the toothpicks, cotton swabs, or dried pasta for bones. **Glue** them onto a piece of construction paper.

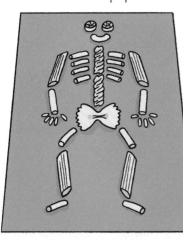

2. **Add** cotton balls, tissues, or construction paper on top of the bones, like skin. **Name** your skeleton!

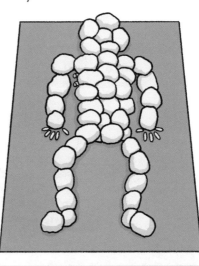

LET'S ENGINEER!

Amelia's crackers often get smashed in her backpack on the way to school.

How can she protect them better?

Design a shell that can protect Amelia's crackers. What materials can cover them? How can you combine or bend the materials to make them stronger?
Test your design.

PROJECT 7 DONE!
Get your sticker!

Animal Babies

All animals have babies. Some lay eggs. Others give birth. Fill in the name of each stage in the life cycle.

egg   hatchling   chick   hen

chicken

Write the numbers 1, 2, 3, and 4 to label the life cycle in order from youngest to oldest.

dog

Some animal babies make noises to let their parents know they need help.

These chirping baby bluebirds are hungry. Draw a line to lead the mother bluebird back to the nest with a worm for her babies to eat.

Some animals don't make noise. How do you think they let their parents know when they need help? How would you let an adult know you needed help without making noise?

_____

People also make noises to communicate.

Write about and draw how you let your parents know when you need something.

_____

_____

_____

Write about and draw how you communicated when you were a baby. Gather information by talking to others in your family.

_____

_____

_____

Young animals can look similar to their parents, but each is still unique.

Draw a line to connect each young shark to its parent.

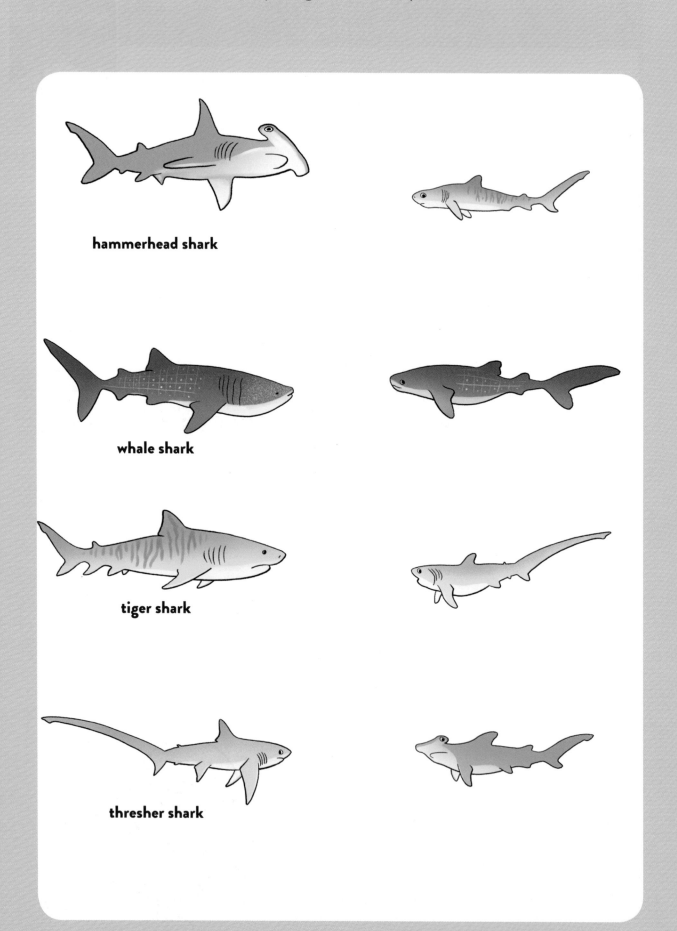

hammerhead shark

whale shark

tiger shark

thresher shark

Look closely at these young animals and their parents.

Circle the parents and babies that look similar. Cross out the parents and babies that look different.

DOG

TAPIR

FROG

ELEPHANT

LET'S START!

GATHER THESE TOOLS AND MATERIALS.

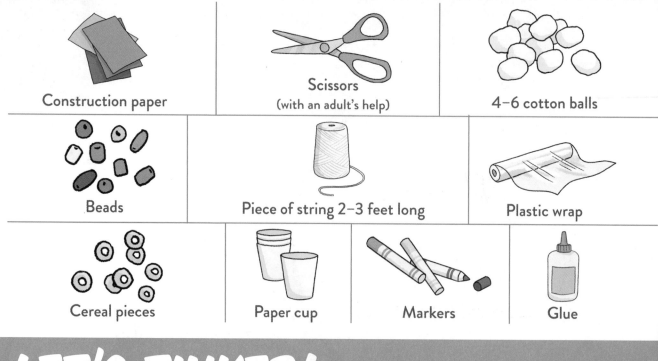

Construction paper	Scissors (with an adult's help)	4–6 cotton balls
Beads	Piece of string 2–3 feet long	Plastic wrap
Cereal pieces	Paper cup	Markers	Glue

LET'S TINKER!

Animals, like some birds, reptiles, and even fish, protect their eggs from the weather and predators in a soft but strong nest.

Look at your materials. Which do you think would be the softest? Which do you think would be the strongest?

Build a nest using your materials. **See** what happens when you put something inside the nest.

LET'S MAKE: BUTTERFLY EGGS!

Many butterflies hide their colorful eggs by laying them on the undersides of leaves. **Make** your own colorful collection of butterfly eggs.

1. Cut a leaf shape out of paper.

2. Create some eggs using cotton balls, beads, or cereal pieces.

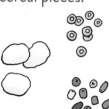

3. Color your eggs with markers if necessary.

4. Glue your eggs to the underside of your paper leaf. **Wait** ten minutes for the glue to dry. **Flip** the leaf over!

LET'S ENGINEER!

Enid is taking apples to school to share with her class. She has a bumpy bus ride and wants to keep her apples safe from bruising.

How can she best protect her apples?

Design a way for Enid to safely carry the apples to school. **Use** some of your materials to represent the apples. How many apples can your design carry?

PROJECT 8 DONE!
Get your sticker!

Animal Survival

Some animals have special body parts that help them get the food and water they need.

Chameleons use their long, skinny tongues to catch insects to eat. Their tongues can be up to two times as long as their bodies! Draw the chameleon's tongue.

Woodpeckers have strong bills and sticky tongues to dig insects from deep inside of trees. Draw the woodpecker's tongue.

Try using your tongue to grab food!

Circle the body part that you predict the hummingbird uses to get nectar from a daylily flower.

Circle the body part that you predict the giraffe uses to reach acacia leaves in tall trees.

Some animals also have special body parts that help them see, hear, move, and protect themselves.

Porcupines are covered in sharp quills to protect them from predators like bobcats, wolves, and owls. Draw the porcupine's quills.

Rhinoceroses have cup-shaped ears that can turn to listen in any direction! This helps them hear sounds from far away. Draw the rhinoceros's ears.

Circle the body part that you predict the elephant uses for making noise.

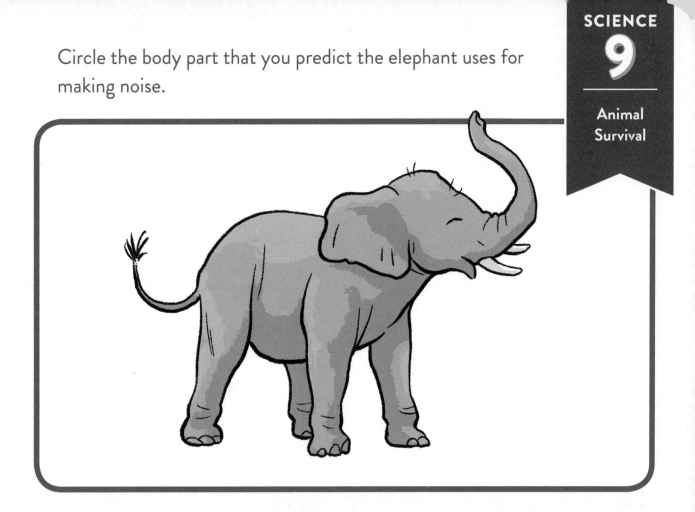

Circle the body part that you predict the turtle uses to walk on land and swim quickly in the water.

People can learn from animals and how they use their special body parts to survive.

Look at how this painted turtle buries himself in the sand and mud when he wants to go to sleep.

Write about and draw how you could go to sleep when it is too bright in your room.

_____

_____

_____

Look at how these arctic bumblebees shiver and move in order to warm up in the cold.

Write about and draw how you could keep warm in the cold.

LET'S START!

GATHER THESE TOOLS AND MATERIALS.

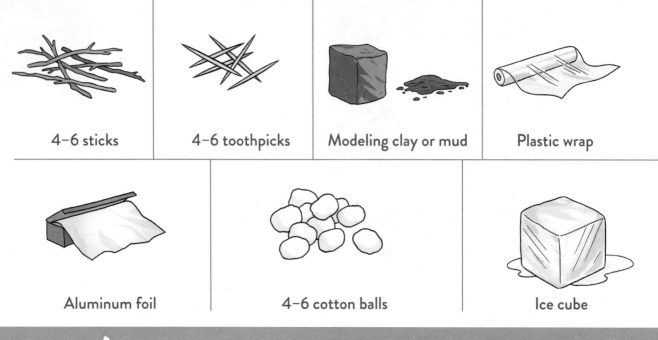

4–6 sticks	4–6 toothpicks	Modeling clay or mud	Plastic wrap
Aluminum foil	4–6 cotton balls	Ice cube	

LET'S TINKER!

Many animals use special body parts to get the food they need. An elephant uses its trunk to lift food to its mouth, and a butterfly uses its proboscis, a special feeding tube, to drink nectar.

Look at your materials. Which can you use to move things, grab things, and pick things up? Which can you use to push or pull with?

LET'S MAKE: COLD PROTECTOR!

Many animals survive in the cold by having layers of fat or blubber or thick fur. **Experiment** to see which materials protect you from the cold.

1. **Grab** a piece of plastic wrap and an ice cube. **Lay** the plastic wrap on your palm (like skin). **Place** the ice cube on the plastic wrap. What does it feel like? How does the feeling change the longer you hold the ice?

2. Choose a layer of protection for your hand, like a lump of clay or some cotton balls. Then **lay** the plastic wrap over it. **Place** the ice on the plastic wrap again, this time with the layer of protection between your hand and the ice. What does it feel like? How does it compare to when you held the ice with no protection?

3. Experiment with different materials from around your home, like a sweater, paper towels, or even feathers. Which ones protect you from the cold the best?

LET'S ENGINEER!

Callie is caught in a hailstorm, and the hail really hurts! (Hail is small clumps of ice and snow that fall like rain.)

How can she protect herself?

Design a protective layer for Callie. How can your materials be used to protect her from the hail?

PROJECT 9 DONE!
Get your sticker!

Five Senses

People have five senses to help them experience their environment. You can hear, see, taste, touch, and smell.

Draw a line to answer each question.

What body part do you use to hear your friend talking?

What body part do you use to see your homework?

What body part do you use to taste a snack?

What body part do you use to touch a friendly pet?

What body part do you use to smell a flower?

You taste with your tongue. Circle the tastes that you like.

Draw on the plate the foods that are your favorite to taste.

You smell with your nose. Draw a line to connect each thing to the words "good smell" or "bad smell."

good smell

bad smell

What is your favorite smell? Draw it.

Your ears help you hear if sounds are loud or soft.
Write the word "loud" or "soft" under each picture.

You touch things with the skin on your hands and on the rest of your body.

Draw a line to connect each picture to a word that describes how it feels.

rough   **cold**   **soft**

Cross out the pictures of things you shouldn't touch.

You see with your eyes. The iris of an eyeball can be many different colors. Color this iris to match yours.

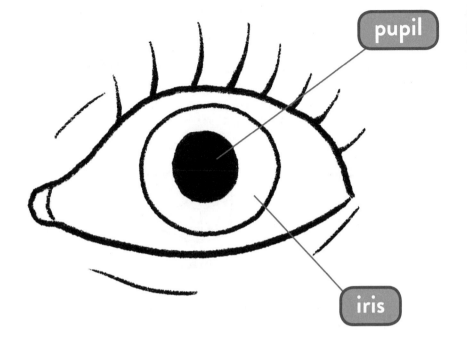

pupil

iris

Look around the room you're in. Draw a picture of what you see.

GATHER THESE TOOLS AND MATERIALS.

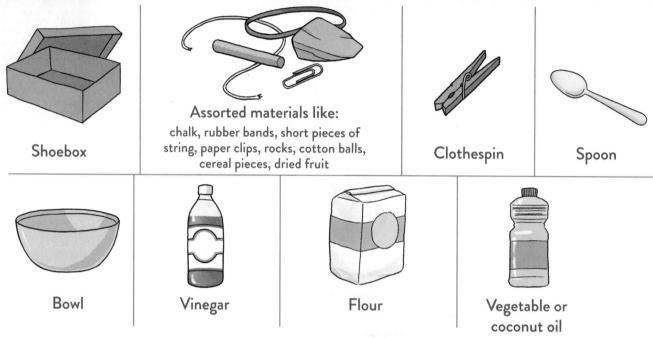

Shoebox

Assorted materials like:
chalk, rubber bands, short pieces of string, paper clips, rocks, cotton balls, cereal pieces, dried fruit

Clothespin

Spoon

Bowl

Vinegar

Flour

Vegetable or coconut oil

LET'S TINKER!

Use your five senses to explore your materials.

Describe what each one feels, looks, sounds, and smells like. Are any safe to taste?

Can you **change** how any of them look, feel, smell, or sound when you hold or combine them?

LET'S MAKE: SENSORY SAND!

Make a mixture to explore with your senses!

1. Pour four cups of flour and ½ cup of oil into a bowl.

2. Mix the flour and oil with a spoon or your hands until it is fully combined.

3. Use your senses to explore!

4. Record your findings on this chart:

	What does the mixture look like?
	What does it sound like?
	What does it feel like?
	What does it smell like?
	Ask an adult if it is safe to taste. If so, what does it taste like?

LET'S ENGINEER!

The MotMots are going on a field trip to the orange orchard, but Amelia doesn't like the smell of oranges.

How can she go on the trip without having to smell the oranges?

Design something to safely block her sense of smell using your materials.

Test your design with different smells.

PROJECT 10 DONE!
Get your sticker!

Energy

Anything that moves uses energy. Light, sound, and heat are forms of energy. Circle the items below that use energy.

Anything that moves uses energy.

Anything that lights up uses energy.

Anything that heats up uses energy.

Anything that makes noise uses energy.

Energy can make things move and change. Read the story aloud.
Circle the main type of energy Callie uses in each picture.

Callie loves camp! She swims in the lake.

light   movement   sound   heat

She plays songs with her friends.

light   movement   sound   heat

She roasts a snack over the campfire.

| light | movement | sound | heat |

She reads under the stars using a flashlight.

| light | movement | sound | heat |

There is energy all around us. Take a walk inside or outside your home and look for things that use energy.

Write about and draw something that lights up.

Write about and draw something that makes noise.

Write about and draw something that moves.

Write about and draw something that heats up.

LET'S START!

GATHER THESE TOOLS AND MATERIALS.

Paper

Dice

Paper towel tube

4–6 cotton balls

Markers or crayons

LET'S TINKER!

When things are in motion, they're using energy.

Move your materials around to see what they're like when they are in motion. What happens when you drop, push, or pull them? Which materials can roll and which can bounce? What is moving these objects?

LET'S MAKE: LIGHT MAP!

1. Draw a map of your home with markers or crayons on a piece of paper.

2. Add the sources of light that keep your home bright. You can **use** stickers from page 387 or draw them with your markers or crayons.

3. When it's dark out, **turn** the lights off.

Is there still some light? If so, where is the light coming from? **Add** any other sources of light that you've noticed to your map.

Do you use the same sources of light during the day and at night?

LET'S ENGINEER!

Enid's art project turned into a mess, and fast. She wants to move her markers off the table to keep them clean, but her hands are covered in paint!

How can Enid move the markers without touching them?

Design a tool to get the markers off the table without touching them with your hands.

PROJECT 11 DONE!
Get your sticker!

Sound

Sound is a form of energy you can hear.

Draw how Dimitri can experiment with each of these things to make sound.

Sound is made when something vibrates. The vibrations make sound waves that move through the air.

Circle the part of the guitar that vibrates to make sound.

Inside your throat, your vocal cords vibrate to make sound, too. Circle the vocal cords that are vibrating.

Write about or draw what this person might be saying.

Sounds have a volume. They can be loud or soft.

Circle the sounds that are usually quiet.

What do you think makes the loudest sound on this page?

_____

Why do you think it needs to be loud? _____

_____

_____

Listen to the sounds around you right now. Then write about and draw what you hear. Think of as many as you can.

_____

_____

_____

Circle the sound that is the loudest.

Put a box around the sound that is the closest to you.

Is the loudest sound also the one closest to you?

_____

_____

Sounds travel at different speeds through different materials. This can change the way something sounds.

Write a description of the sound you would hear in each picture. Then circle the sound in each row you predict would be louder.

Drop your pencil on this book.
Next drop your pencil on the floor.
Write about and draw which sound was quieter.

Find another surface where you can experiment with dropping the pencil—
maybe a table, a carpet, or a chair. Write about and draw what you hear.

LET'S START!

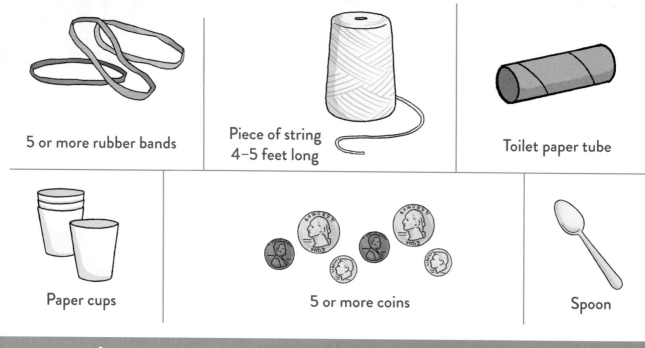

5 or more rubber bands

Piece of string 4–5 feet long

Toilet paper tube

Paper cups

5 or more coins

Spoon

LET'S TINKER!

Pick up each of your materials. What sounds can you make with them?

Tap each one on the floor, on your leg, and on a table. Does the sound change? What happens if you combine materials?

Think about how you can use your materials to make other noises. Can you make sounds that are softer or louder?

Touch your throat while you hum or sing. Can you feel your vocal cords vibrating? Do any of your materials vibrate?

LET'S MAKE: SOUND OBSERVER!

All sounds are made when something vibrates. **Make** a tool to carry vibrations right to your ears!

1. Tie the middle of a long piece of string around a metal spoon.

2. Wrap the ends of the string a few times around your two index fingers, then **stick** your fingers into your ears.

3. Experiment with swinging the spoon gently into objects around you. The string is carrying vibrations from the spoon right to your fingers and into your eardrums! What does it sound like? Do hard and soft objects make different kinds of sounds? How does the sound change when you swing the spoon gently? How about quickly?

LET'S ENGINEER!

Brian has been busy cooking a special meal for his family. Now it's time for dinner, but his dinner bell is broken.

How can Brian let everyone know that it's time to eat—without using his voice?

Build an instrument Brian can play to call his family to dinner.

PROJECT 12 DONE!
Get your sticker!

Light

Light is a form of energy you can see. Some things give off their own light. Color those things yellow.

Some things can only be seen with a light source.

Draw a light source you use in your room at night.

Draw how your room looks.

Draw a light source you use in your room during the day.

Draw how your room looks.

Look around the space you are in. What light source is closest to you?

Light moves in a straight line. Draw beams of light from each of the three light sources in the picture.

Read the story aloud. Then add details to the picture showing what you think Brian saw under the bed.

It was very late and dark at the sleepover. All of Brian's friends were sleeping. Brian heard a noise in the dark. Then he heard it again! Brian got his flashlight out of his backpack. He snuck over to the bed and slowly peeked underneath it. Then he flipped on his flashlight!

Many kinds of balls bounce.

Draw how you think this ball will bounce.

When a beam of light hits a shiny surface, like a mirror, it also bounces. This is called reflection.

Draw how you think the light of the flashlight will reflect.

You can use a mirror to redirect a beam of light. You can also see your reflection.

Stand in front of a mirror in your home. Draw what you see.

Circle the shiny things that can reflect light.

LET'S START! GATHER THESE TOOLS AND MATERIALS.

Flashlight	Pencil, crayon, or marker	Construction paper	Scissors (with an adult's help)	Tape
Aluminum foil	Spoon	4–6 twist ties	Clothes hanger	3-5 pieces of string, each 1–2 feet long

LET'S TINKER!

Look at your materials and predict which ones will reflect light.

Use the flashlight to shine a beam of light onto each item. Which items reflect the light? How can you tell? Were your predictions correct?

Turn all the lights off. Does anything change?

Discover other materials in your home that reflect light.

LET'S MAKE: FLASHLIGHT PICTURES!

1. **Place** your flashlight facedown first on a piece of paper. **Trace** it with a pencil, crayon, or marker to make a circle.

2. **Cut** out the paper circle. Then **cut** out or **poke** a few holes in the circle.

3. Tape the paper circle over the lens of the flashlight and turn it on. **Point** the flashlight at the wall, floor, or ceiling to project your pattern!

LET'S ENGINEER!

It's time for Amelia's party, but she doesn't have a disco ball. A disco ball reflects light around a room in fun shapes and patterns! Amelia can't have a party without something like a disco ball.

How can you help save the day with a similar decoration?

Build your own hanging party decoration that reflects light in fun shapes and patterns.

PROJECT 13 DONE!
Get your sticker!

Shadows

Some materials allow a lot of light to pass through them. Other materials allow only a little light to pass through them.

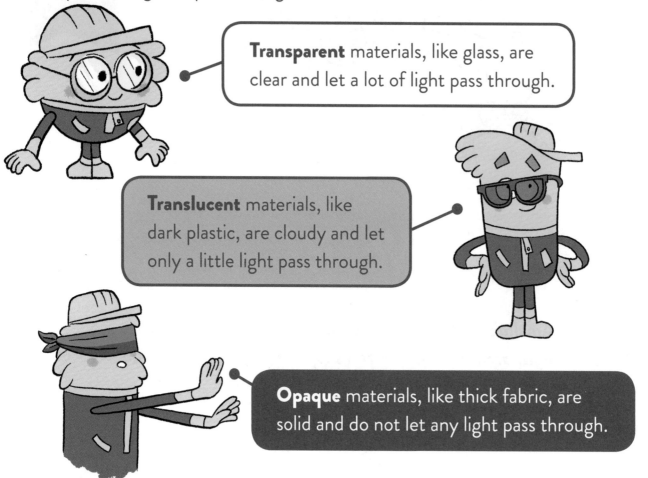

Transparent materials, like glass, are clear and let a lot of light pass through.

Translucent materials, like dark plastic, are cloudy and let only a little light pass through.

Opaque materials, like thick fabric, are solid and do not let any light pass through.

Draw what you see when you look through a pair of sunglasses.

Look around your home. What other translucent materials do you see? Try looking through them!

Draw what you think the flashlight's light rays will do when they hit these objects. Then circle whether each one is transparent, translucent, or opaque.

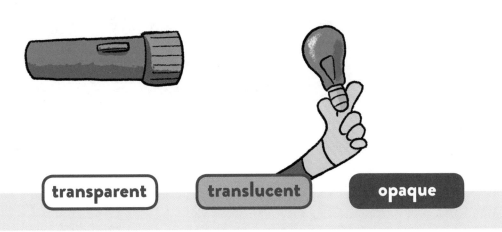

transparent   **translucent**   **opaque**

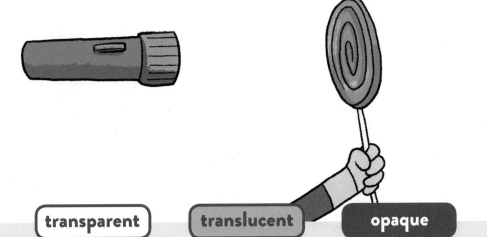

transparent   **translucent**   **opaque**

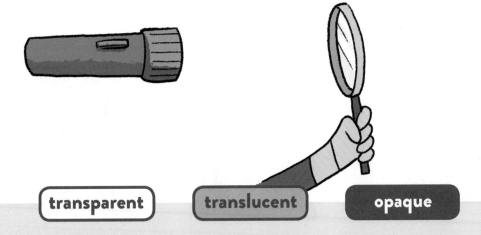

transparent   **translucent**   **opaque**

A shadow is made when light is blocked by an opaque object. Read the poem aloud. Then draw a shadow behind each MotMot and decorate it.

Shadow, shadow, on the wall,
who's the funniest of them all?
Shadows short and shadows tall,
watch them dance until nightfall.

Look around your home. What other opaque materials do you see? Try making shadows with them on this page!

Shadows create shade, which helps to keep the area in the shadows cool.

The MotMots are playing outside on a hot day. Draw the shadows in each picture that will keep the MotMots cool.

Should the MotMots choose the sun or the shade?
Circle one word below.

sun

shade

sun

shade

Take a walk around the inside or outside of your home and find a place where you can make a shadow.

What light source will you use?

_____

What does your shadow look like?

_____

Flashlight	Paper	Aluminum foil	Toilet paper tube

Plastic wrap	4–6 cotton balls	Collection of toy animals, action figures, or dolls

LET'S TINKER!

Hold your materials in front of a flashlight or a sunny window one at a time. Can you make shadows with them? Do the shadows move? Do any of the materials not make shadows?

Move the materials close to the light, then far away from it. How do the shadows change?

Combine the materials and see what happens.

Think about other light sources you can use to make shadows.

LET'S MAKE: SHADOW SHOW!

1. Make a shadow shape of an animal or a person with your materials or hands.

2. Use a light source like a flashlight or a sunny window to project your shadow character onto the floor or wall.

3. Move your shadow character around.

4. Make other shadow shapes to create a story with your shadow character. **Combine** the materials to make shadows of different shapes and sizes. **Try** making more than one shadow at a time.

LET'S ENGINEER!

The MotMots are having a beach party, and Callie has a special delivery for them. However, she doesn't know where to land her hot-air balloon.

How can Callie figure out where to land?

Design a solution with your materials to make a shadow **X** on the ground where Callie can land.

PROJECT 14 DONE!
Get your sticker!

Light & Sound

Light and sound can be used to communicate with other people, even from far away. Circle the things you've seen and/or heard.

lighthouse

fire engine

ambulance

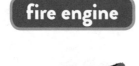

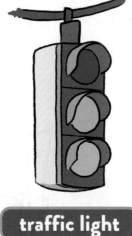

traffic light

bell

dog

Look around your home. What do you see that makes light or sound?

Fill in the diagram with the objects from page 242 that fall into each category. Which ones communicate with light, with sound, or with both light and sound?

Ways to Communicate

signal wands

fire alarm

light

light and sound

sound

yelling

People use sound to communicate in many ways.

Circle the pictures of the MotMots communicating using sound.

Draw a picture of how you communicate using sound.

Many animals communicate using sound, too.

Read the poem aloud. Then draw a picture of how a rattlesnake communicates.

Rattlesnake Shake

A rattlesnake has no ears you can see,
so it cannot hear like you or like me.
But it still uses sound as it slithers around
to scare predators in the air and on the ground.

When an eagle, coyote, or whip snake comes by,
this snake will hold its rattle up high.
The sound of its shaker says, "Do not come near!"
And those who hear should soon disappear.

People also use light to communicate in many ways.
Write a ✓ under "yes" or "no" for each item in the chart.

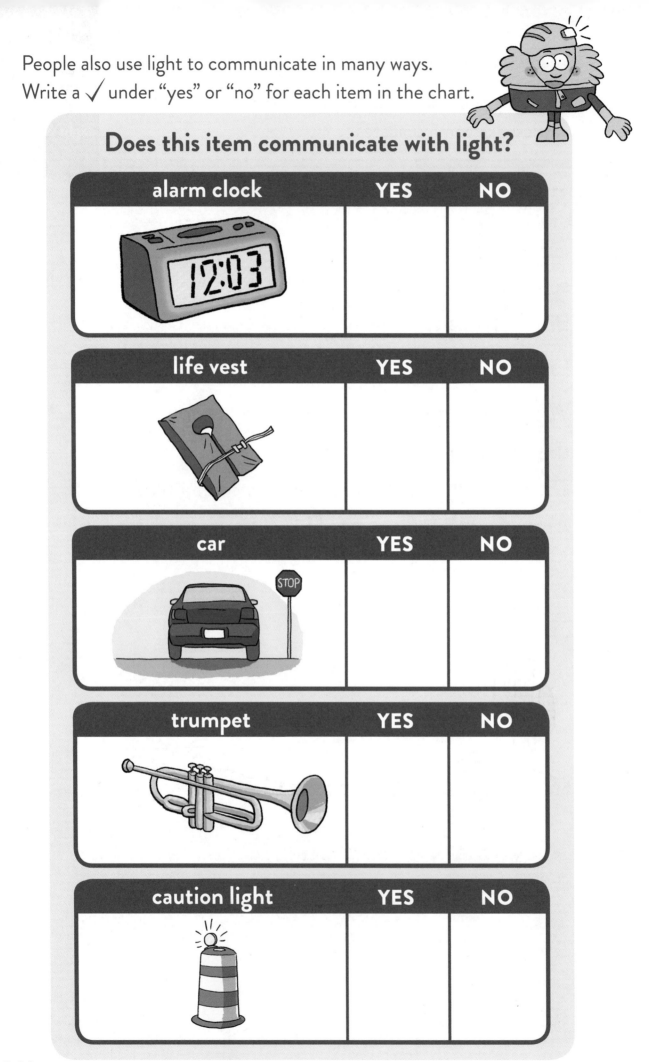

Does this item communicate with light?

alarm clock	YES	NO

life vest	YES	NO

car	YES	NO

trumpet	YES	NO

caution light	YES	NO

Traffic lights communicate important information.

 means **GO** and means **STOP**.

Trace a line through the maze to the movie theater. Drive only on roads with a .

LET'S START!

GATHER THESE TOOLS AND MATERIALS.

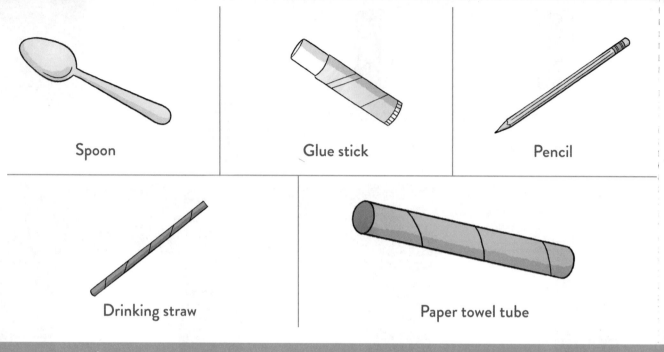

Spoon

Glue stick

Pencil

Drinking straw

Paper towel tube

LET'S TINKER!

Tap each of your materials on a table, on the floor, and on one another. What sounds can you make? Are your sounds loud or soft?

Play around to create your own pattern with sounds. Which sounds repeat?

LET'S MAKE: SECRET CODE!

Many of the ways that we communicate use patterns.

1. **Create** your own secret code using sound patterns.

2. Use the chart below to keep track of your sound patterns.

Sound	Sound	Sound	Sound
1 loud tap	3 quiet claps		
Meaning	Meaning	Meaning	Meaning

LET'S ENGINEER!

Frank is going to the movie theater with his mom. He knows that he's not allowed to talk while the movie is playing, but he may get hungry or thirsty before it's over.

How can Frank tell his mom what he needs without talking?

Design an object for Frank to take in his pocket to communicate.

Or **think** of a way he can communicate with just his body.

PROJECT 15 DONE!
Get your sticker!

ANSWER KEY

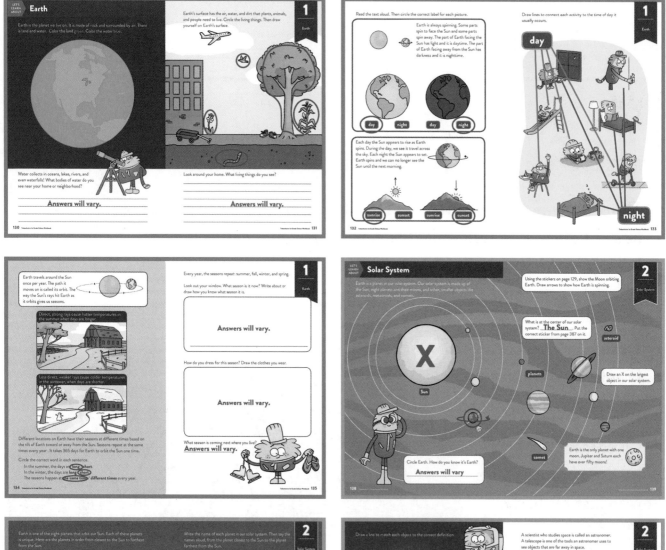

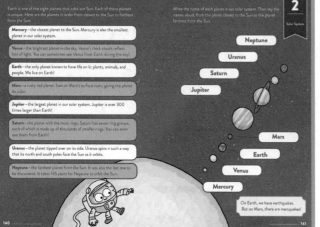

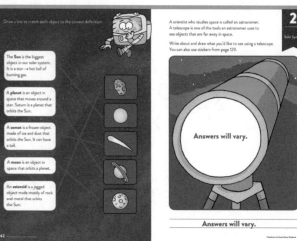

Sun, Moon & Stars

There is only one star in our solar system—the Sun. It is a ball of burning gases that provides the light and heat we need to survive on Earth. Even though it is far away, the Sun is so bright that we cannot look directly at it. Its rays are so powerful that we have to protect our skin so it doesn't burn.

Circle the things you use to protect yourself from the Sun's rays.

The Sun is always shining, but we cannot always see it because Earth spins. When the part of Earth that we are on is facing the Sun, it is day. When the part of Earth that we are on rotates away from the Sun, it is night.

Color the side of Earth reached by the Sun's rays yellow. Color the side of Earth that no light is reaching.

Read the poem aloud.

Phases of the Moon

Some planets have many moons
and some have none.
On Earth we are lucky—
we have one!

Our moon circles Earth
on a month-long path.
We call this an orbit—
now comes the math.

The Sun shines upon the Moon
and lights up different places.
Each new look has a name—
we call them the Moon's phases!

A full moon shows its whole face.
A new moon hides its light.
A half-moon is half shadowed,
while the other half is bright.

The Moon is waxing when it's growing
and waning when it's not.
It's crescent when there's less than half
And gibbous when there's a lot.

The phase of the Moon is always changing,
and now that you know the reasons,
you can watch and track the patterns,
even through the seasons!

Color the phases of the Moon that we see from Earth. Use yellow to color the parts of the Moon lit up by the Sun. Use ___ to color the parts of the Moon we cannot see.

half
gibbous
crescent
full
new
gibbous
crescent
half

Look out your window at night. Can you see the Moon? Which phase is it in?
Answers will vary.

Stars are balls of burning gases. Groups of stars in a pattern can form a constellation. Connect the dots to form constellations.

Draw what you see outside your window at night. Can you find a constellation? If so, draw it. If not, draw your own pattern of stars.

Answers will vary.

Parts of a Plant

Plants have different parts that help them live and grow.

Roots collect water and nutrients, and they hold the plant firmly in the ground.

A **stem** or **trunk** holds the plant or tree up and transports water and nutrients to the leaves, flowers, and fruits.

Leaves collect sunlight and make food for the plant. They also make oxygen.

Flowers grow seeds for the plant.

Fruits provide protection for the seeds. They also help spread the seeds through wind, water, or animals.

leaves
flower
stem
fruit
roots

What plants do you see inside or outside your home?

Label the parts of the plants in Brian's garden.

leaves
fruit
trunk
flower
stem
roots

Which parts can you see on the plants near you?

Plants use their different parts to help them live and grow in different habitats.

Connect each plant to its habitat.

Bearberry plants have dark leaves and low stems. This helps them absorb heat from the Sun and from Earth so they can survive in very cold temperatures.

Agave leaves have a waxy coating to protect the water inside the plant. This helps them survive in hot habitats with little rainfall.

Bromeliads grow on other plants instead of in the ground. This helps them get closer to the Sun when the plants around them are tall.

Water lilies have stems and leaves that can bend and move. This helps them live in underwater habitats.

RAIN FOREST
FRESH WATER
DESERT
TUNDRA

Look at how each plant uses its parts to live and grow. Then design your own solution to each problem.

A peanut shell protects the seeds inside.

Write about and draw a solution you can use to protect your lunch on the way to school.

Answers will vary.

A tree's branches hold the leaves up high to get light from the Sun.

Write about and draw a solution you can use to hold a wet swimsuit and towel up to the Sun to dry.

Answers will vary.

Plant Growth

Plants are living things. They need light, air, water, and nutrients from the dirt to live and grow. Help Dimitri water his plants with the watering can. Draw a line through the maze to visit each plant.

Plants all need the same things to live, whether they are growing indoors or outdoors. Color each plant's light source yellow. Color each plant's water source blue. Color each plant's nutrients source brown.

What are other ways that plants can get the water they need to survive?

Answers will vary.

Plants respond to changes in their environment to keep getting the things they need to live and grow. Draw how each plant changes to meet its needs.

Answers will vary.

The kapok tree needs lots of light, so it grows taller than the trees around it to gather more sunlight. Draw the tree taller.

Answers will vary.

The spruce tree needs water. During a drought, when there is very little rain, the roots grow deeper to find the water the tree needs. Draw the roots deeper.

Answers will vary.

The tulip plant needs its pollen to make seeds, so it closes its petals to protect its pollen when it rains. Draw a tulip plant closed.

Answers will vary.

This indoor fern needs sunlight, so it grows toward the window to get more light. Draw the fern's leaves growing closer to the window.

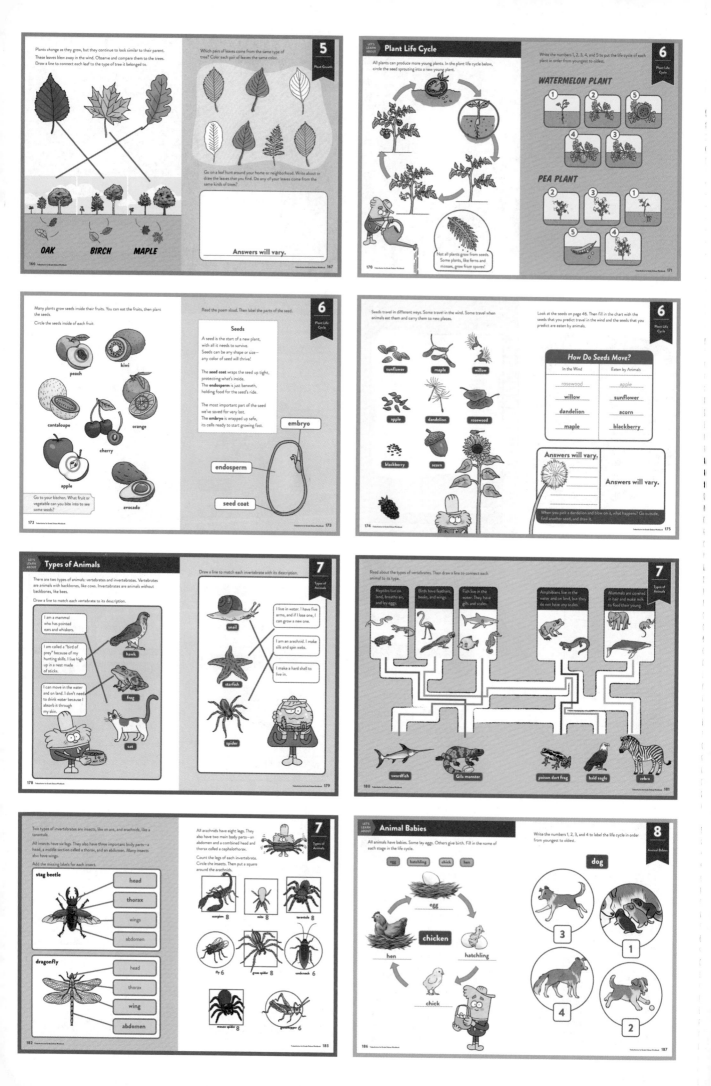

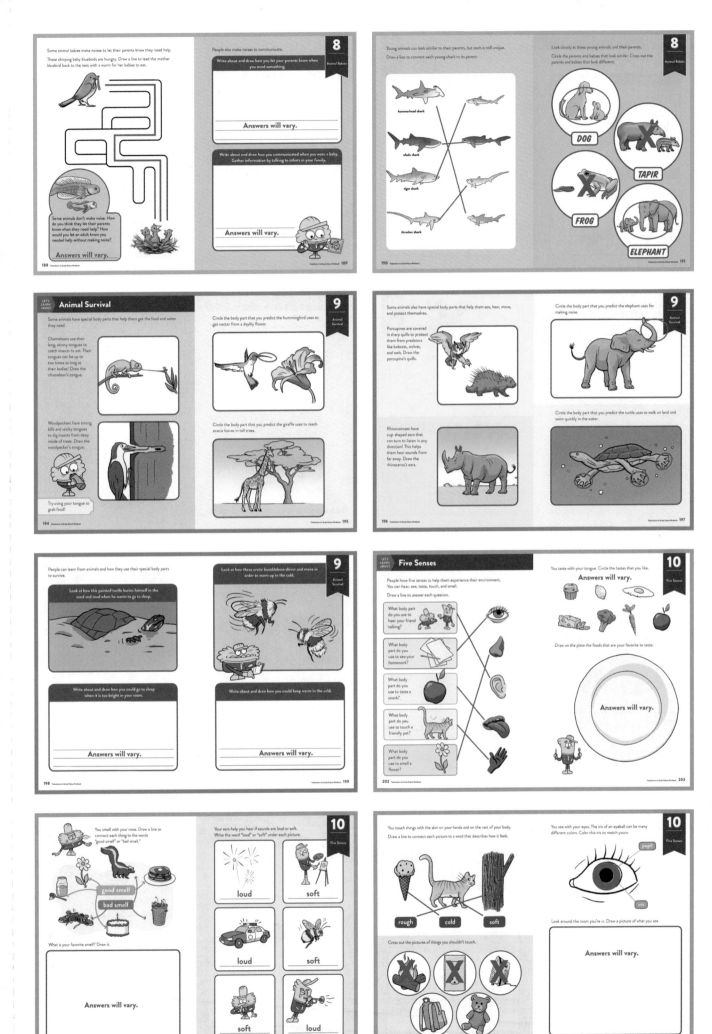

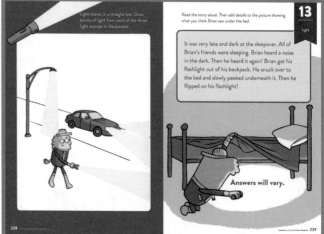

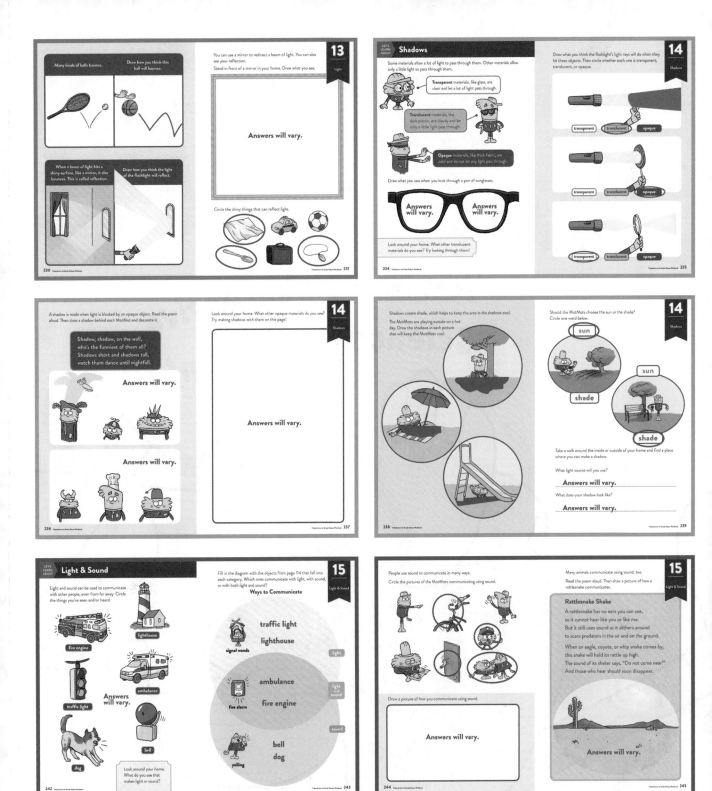

Spread (pages 230–231)

Many kinds of balls bounce.

Draw how you think this ball will bounce.

When a beam of light hits a shiny surface, like a mirror, it also bounces. This is called reflection.

Draw how you think the light of the flashlight will reflect.

You can use a mirror to redirect a beam of light. You can also see your reflection.

Stand in front of a mirror in your home. Draw what you see.

Answers will vary.

Circle the shiny things that can reflect light.

Spread (pages 234–235)

Shadows

Some materials allow a lot of light to pass through them. Other materials allow only a little light to pass through them.

Transparent materials, like glass, are clear and let a lot of light pass through.

Translucent materials, like dark plastic, are cloudy and let only a little light pass through.

Opaque materials, like thick fabric, are solid and do not let any light pass through.

Draw what you see when you look through a pair of sunglasses.

Answers will vary.   Answers will vary.

Look around your home. What other translucent materials do you see? Try looking through them!

Draw what you think the flashlight's light rays will do when they hit these objects. Then circle whether each one is transparent, translucent, or opaque.

transparent   translucent   opaque

transparent   translucent   opaque

transparent   translucent   opaque

Spread (pages 236–237)

A shadow is made when light is blocked by an opaque object. Read the poem aloud. Then draw a shadow behind each MotMot and decorate it.

Shadow, shadow, on the wall,
who's the funniest of them all?
Shadows short and shadows tall,
watch them dance until nightfall.

Answers will vary.

Answers will vary.

Look around your home. What other opaque materials do you see? Try making shadows with them on this page!

Answers will vary.

Spread (pages 238–239)

Shadows create shade, which helps to keep the area in the shadows cool.

The MotMots are playing outside on a hot day. Draw the shadows in each picture that will keep the MotMots cool.

Should the MotMots choose the sun or the shade? Circle one word below.

sun

sun

shade

shade

Take a walk around the inside or outside of your home and find a place where you can make a shadow.

What light source will you use?

Answers will vary.

What does your shadow look like?

Answers will vary.

Spread (pages 242–243)

Light & Sound

Light and sound can be used to communicate with other people, even from far away. Circle the things you've seen and/or heard.

fire engine

lighthouse

ambulance

Answers will vary.

traffic light

bell

dog

Look around your home. What do you see that makes light or sound?

Fill in the diagram with the objects from page 114 that fall into each category. Which ones communicate with light, with sound, or with both light and sound?

Ways to Communicate

signal wands

fire alarm

yelling

traffic light
lighthouse

ambulance
fire engine

bell
dog

light

light and sound

sound

Spread (pages 244–245)

People use sound to communicate in many ways. Circle the pictures of the MotMots communicating using sound.

Draw a picture of how you communicate using sound.

Answers will vary.

Many animals communicate using sound, too. Read the poem aloud. Then draw a picture of how a rattlesnake communicates.

Rattlesnake Shake

A rattlesnake has no ears you can see,
so it cannot hear like you or like me.
But it still uses sound as it slithers around
to scare predators in the air and on the ground.

When an eagle, coyote, or whip snake comes by,
this snake will hold its rattle up high.
The sound of its shaker says, "Do not come near!"
And those who hear should soon disappear.

Answers will vary.

Spread (pages 246–247)

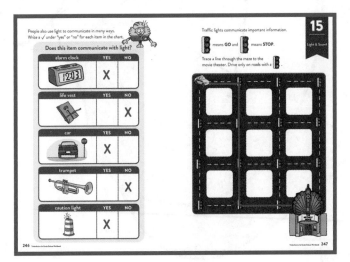

People also use light to communicate in many ways. Write a ✓ under "yes" or "no" for each item in the chart.

Does this item communicate with light?

	YES	NO
alarm clock		X
life vest		X
car	X	
trumpet		X
caution light	X	

Traffic lights communicate important information.

means **GO** and   means **STOP**.

Trace a line through the maze to the movie theater. Drive only on roads with a [green light].

1ST GRADE · ENGLISH LANGUAGE ARTS · AGES 6–7

by Megan Hewes Butler

illustrated by Taryn Johnson

educational consulting by Mindy Yip

 Odd Dot · New York

A **fictional text** describes imaginary events and people. With the help of an adult, read this fiction story aloud.

The Tag Sale

Honk, honk! Today was Brian and Amelia's tag sale. Amelia squeezed her old bicycle horn to let all the neighbors know. Brian hung a big sign in his front yard. Amelia put price tags on a drum and a sled. Brian put price tags on a bat, a sock, and a toy ship.

Soon their neighbors arrived. Brian's friend Zed bought a flag for his tree house for one dollar. Amelia's teacher bought a toy car tire for twenty-five cents.

At the end of the day, Brian and Amelia had sold everything! They counted the money—they had earned ten dollars and thirty cents! Amelia wanted to throw an ice cream party. Brian wanted a new swing.

In the end, they agreed to give the money to Tinker Town's animal shelter. When they went to the shelter with their donation, Amelia and Brian got to play with all the animals!

Draw a line to lead Amelia and Brian to the animal shelter.
Start at A and follow the letters in alphabetical order to Z.
Trace each letter as you go.

A B C D E I

F

P L K J I H G L

M

J

N K

O P Q R S T W

U

R

V Y

S W

X U

T

Y Z

A, E, I, O, and U are vowels.
Circle the vowels.

Write each missing uppercase letter.

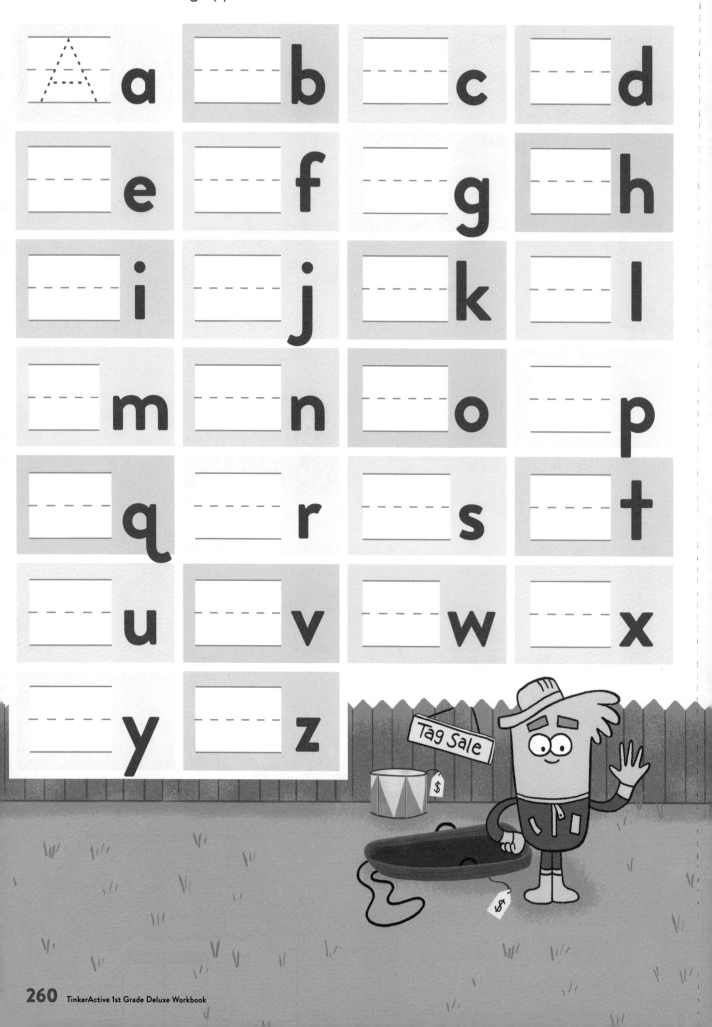

A a   b   c   d

e   f   g   h

i   j   k   l

m   n   o   p

q   r   s   t

u   v   w   x

y   z

Tag Sale

Write each missing lowercase letter.

A a   B   C

D   E   F   G

H   I   J   K

L   M   N   O

P   Q   R   S

T   U   V   W

X   Y   Z

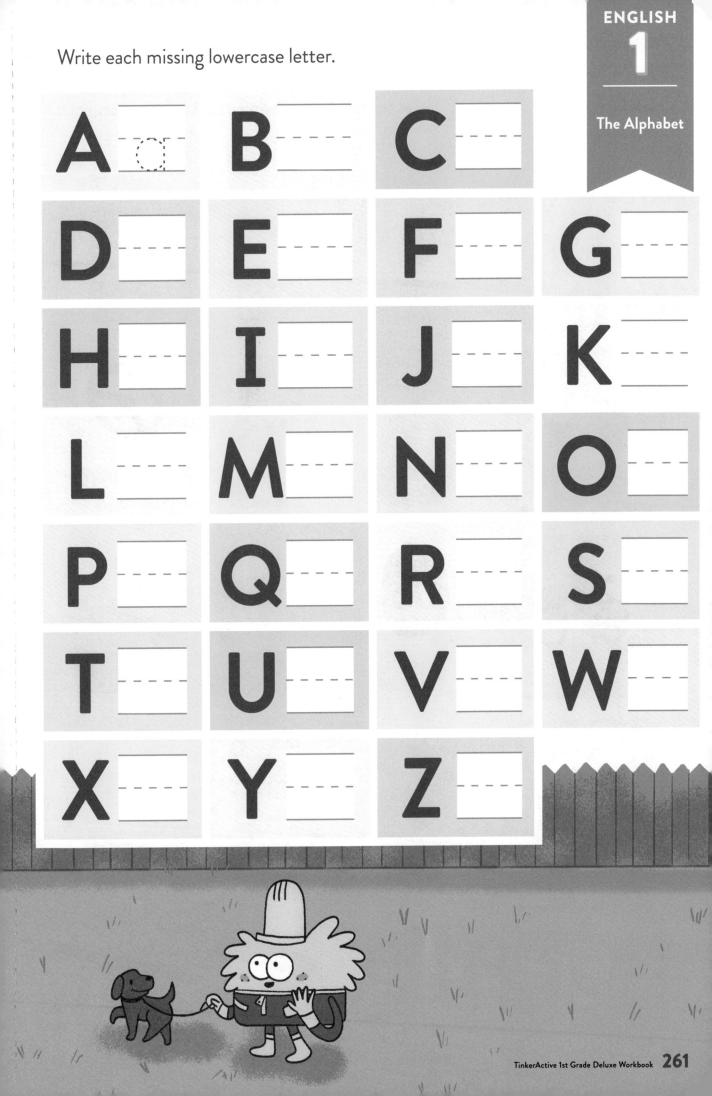

Vowels can make different sounds. **Long vowels** sound just like their names—like the e's in bee!

Read each word with a long vowel sound aloud. Then circle the other objects with long vowels.

cage · lace · bat · paint

bee · pen · leaf · wheel

bike · tire · pie · ship

rose · coat · lock · bow

glue · mug · tube · flute

Short vowels make a different sound—they don't sound like their names.

Read each word with a short vowel sound aloud. Then circle the objects with short vowels.

map	flag	clay	fan
net	teeth	bell	sled
wig	dish	dice	bin
sock	bone	mop	frog
cup	bus	drum	cube

LET'S START! GATHER THESE TOOLS AND MATERIALS.

10 or more drinking straws—preferably a large size	String	Scissors (with an adult's help)
Permanent marker	Pencils	4–6 cotton swabs

LET'S TINKER!

Make the shape of the capital letter A with your materials. Next, **try** B. How many letters of the alphabet can you make? Can you make uppercase and lowercase letters? Can you spell your name?

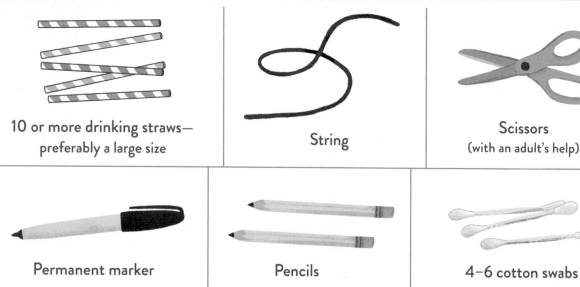

LET'S MAKE: ALPHABET GAME!

1. Cut drinking straws into pieces about the length of your thumb. **Make** 26 pieces.

2. Flatten one straw piece and write the letter A on it with a permanent marker. **Write** the letter B on another piece. **Keep going** until you've written the entire alphabet.

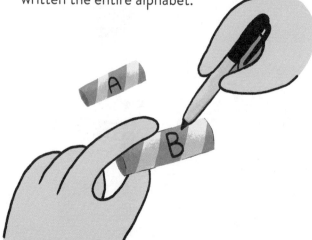

3. Thread the straws onto a piece of string in alphabetical order, starting with A.

4. When all 26 are on, **cut** the string and tie the ends into a knot to make a loop.

5. Starting with A, **find** an object in your home that starts with that letter: like an apple or your ankle! Then **slide** to the next letter on the string: B. **Find** an object in your home that starts with every letter of the alphabet! How many rounds can you complete without repeating objects?

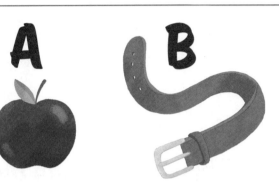

LET'S ENGINEER!

Callie is having her own tag sale. She has two tables: a short vowel table and a long vowel table. So far, the short vowel table is empty.

How can she make some items with short vowels for her tag sale?

Use your materials to make items with short vowels. Can you make a wig or a ring? What about a map or a hat? What other short vowel items can you make?

PROJECT 1: DONE!
Get your sticker!

Phonics

A **limerick** is a poem that has five lines that rhyme in a pattern and is funny. With the help of an adult, read the limerick, written by Edward Lear, aloud. Then answer the questions.

There Was an Old Man with a Beard

There was an old man with a beard,

Who said, "It is just as I feared,

Two owls and a hen,

A lark and a wren,

Have all built their nests in my beard!"

Which word rhymes with **beard**?

_____

- - - - - - - - - - - - - - - - - -

_____

Which word rhymes with **hen**?

_____

- - - - - - - - - - - - - - - - - -

_____

What is another word you know that rhymes with **hen**?

_____

- - - - - - - - - - - - - - - - - -

_____

Say the sound of each letter. Then read the name of each bird.
Last, trace each word.

jay

gull

crane

duck

tern

crow

Make up your own bird that has made a nest in this beard. Draw a picture
and write its name.

The name of my bird is

_____

_____

_____.

With the help of an adult, read the limerick, written by Edward Lear, aloud.

There Was an Old Man Who Supposed

There was an old man who supposed

That the street door was partially closed;

But some very large rats

Ate his coats and his hats,

While that futile old gentleman dozed.

Which words rhyme with **supposed**?

_____   _____

- - - - - - - - - - - - - -   - - - - - - - - - - - - - -

_____   _____

Which word rhymes with **rats**?

_____

- - - - - - - - - - - -

_____

What is another word you know that rhymes with **rats**?

_____

- - - - - - - - - - - -

_____

Act it out! What did the rats do when they snuck in the door?

A **syllable** is a word, or part of a word, that is pronounced as one beat.

These words have one syllable. Read each word aloud and clap once for the one syllable.

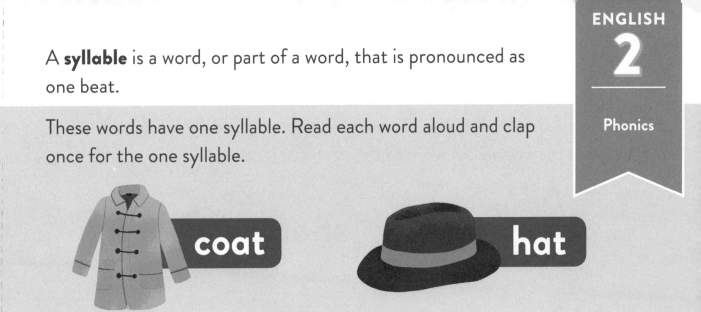

coat

hat

These words have two syllables. Read each word aloud and clap twice for the two syllables.

zipper

swimsuit

Read the name of each object aloud and clap for each syllable. Circle the objects that have only one syllable.

necklace

vest

ring

pajamas

dress

rat

scarf

In some words, two consonants work together to make one sound. This is called a **digraph**.

Read each word aloud. Listen to how each digraph forms one sound. Then draw a line to match each word to the correct picture.

shoes   **sh**irt   **sh**orts   **sh**ovel

si**ng**   ri**ng**   earri**ng**   wi**ng**

In some words, two consonants work together, but each individual sound can still be heard. This is called a **blend**.

Read each word aloud. Listen to how each blend has two sounds. Then draw a line to match each word to the correct picture.

swim   **sw**eatshirt   **sw**eater   **sw**ing

shi**rt**   di**rt**   ski**rt**   hea**rt**

LET'S START!

GATHER THESE TOOLS AND MATERIALS.

Thick paper or cardboard	Markers	Newspaper	Cup	Food coloring	Tablespoon
Spoon	4–6 drinking straws	Pencil	6 or more rubber bands	6 or more twist ties	Tissues

LET'S TINKER!

Hunt for items with one-syllable names, like a pen and a hat. **Look** around your home or find items in your materials. **Clap** to make sure that each item you pick has only one syllable!

pot

bag

LET'S MAKE: BEARD NESTS!

1. Draw a face on a thick sheet of paper, like watercolor paper or cardboard.

2. Lay it on top of a piece of newspaper. This can get messy!

3. Mix 3 drops of one color of food coloring and 1 tablespoon of water in a cup.

4. Use a spoon to add one drop of the colored water to the bottom of the face drawing.

5. Blow through a straw to spread the water and create a beard.

6. You can **try** again with the same color or mix a new color in another cup.

7. When the water is dry, **use** a pencil to add birds to your beard.

LET'S ENGINEER!

Some birds near Dimitri's home don't have a nest. So he wants to build one for them! The problem is that every time he builds one, it falls apart when he lifts it onto a tree branch.

How can he build a nest that won't fall apart when he picks it up?

Use your materials to make a nest. **Test** it by picking it up—does it fall apart or stay together? Which materials work best? As you work, **say** the name of each material you use aloud. Which letter sound does each begin with? Which letter sound does each end with?

PROJECT 2: DONE!
Get your sticker!

Word Building

A **legend** is an old story that has been shared for a long time. Parts of the story may be true, but no one knows for sure. With the help of an adult, read the legend aloud.

Johnny Appleseed

John Chapman was an apple farmer who was born in 1774. As a young man, he traveled the country. He dreamed of planting enough apple trees so that no one would go hungry. There would be apples for everyone in the whole country.

The legend says that John lived outside. He slept on the ground and walked barefoot. He may have worn a scratchy burlap sack for clothes and a cooking pot as a hat! He also carried a leather bag everywhere he went.

John visited mills that made apple cider. He would ask for their extra apple seeds and put them in his bag. As he wandered, he spread apple seeds and returned later to care for the apple trees that had grown.

John met lots of people and made many friends. People called him Johnny Appleseed because of his love for apples. He spread seeds for over fifty years and planted thousands of trees!

Prefixes and suffixes are groups of letters that can be added to a word to make a new word. Knowing prefixes and suffixes can help you figure out unknown words.

Prefixes go at the start of words.

re- means again	un- means not
refill with water means to fill again with water	**uneven row** means a row that is not even

Suffixes go at the end of words.

-ful means full of	-less means without
colorful apples means apples full of color	**seedless grapes** means grapes without seeds

Circle the picture that matches each phrase.

feeling unhappy

painful sting

repainted sign

feeling cheerful

unripe apple

toothless animal

Inflectional endings can be added to the end of words to change their meanings.

-s or -es means more than one	**-ing** means an action is happening now	**-ed** means an action happened in the past
seed**s**	plant**ing**	plant**ed**

Write the inflectional ending for each word.

add **s**	add **ing**	add **ed**
shovel ____	water ____	pick ____
bag ____	fall ____	fix ____
apple ____	eat ____	climb ____

A **root word** is a word without any inflectional endings, prefixes, or suffixes.

plant

(plants) (planting) (planted) (replant)

Read each word aloud and circle the root word.

apples

picking

stems

eating

pears

rewater

growing

rained

When a word ends with a silent **e**, the vowel in front of it usually makes a long vowel sound.

r**a**ke k**i**te s**a**me

When two vowels are next to each other, the first one usually makes a long vowel sound.

r**ai**n fr**ui**t p**ie**

Draw a line through the apple orchard that only passes words with long vowel sounds.

LET'S START!

GATHER THESE TOOLS AND MATERIALS.

2–3 apples	Paint	Paper plate	Paper

Cardboard (from a shipping box or cereal box)	Scissors (with an adult's help)	Markers

LET'S TINKER!

Move your materials according to these verbs:

> **bend   stack   poke   roll   push**

Add re- to these verbs to move your materials again. For example: rebend means to bend again. Then **move** your materials with your own verbs!

LET'S MAKE: APPLE AND SEED PRINTS!

1. With the help of an adult, **cut** the apples in half—some lengthwise and some widthwise.

2. Pour paint onto a paper plate.

3. Press the cut side of an apple into the paint.

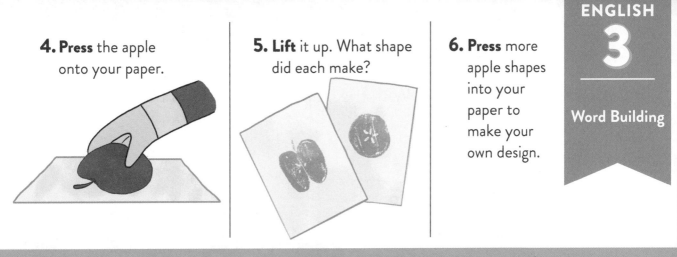

4. Press the apple onto your paper.

5. Lift it up. What shape did each make?

6. Press more apple shapes into your paper to make your own design.

LET'S ENGINEER!

The MotMots made their own word-building game! They put together root words and endings to make word sculptures. Whoever can make the most words wins!

How can each MotMot make as many word sculptures as possible?

Build your own word sculptures. With the help of an adult, **cut** twelve rectangles about the size of your hand from a piece of cardboard. Then **make** four small V-shaped cuts in each one. **Use** four of the rectangles to write each of the following endings:

> -s   -es   -ing   -ed

Now, **write** your root words on the remaining rectangles. **Think** about the things you like to do, such as play or read. What happens when you put the endings on those root words? You can **make** "plays" or "reading." Last, **build** a sculpture with the rectangles. How many words can you make? How big can you make your sculpture?

paint   -s   -ed

-ing

PROJECT 3: DONE!
Get your sticker!

Vocabulary

A **letter** is a written message. With the help of an adult, read the letters aloud.

Dear Ava,

We hope this letter gets to you in Alaska. Is it cold there all the time? Is your new home on an iceberg? Do you ride a dog sled to get to school?

We miss you!

Sincerely,

Ms. Tinkerton's Class

Dear Ms. Tinkerton's class,

Hello from Alaska! It is not cold all the time. During the winter it is dark, cold, and snowy. But during the summer it is warm and sunny. Sometimes I can even wear shorts!

My home is not on an iceberg—it's on green grass. There is some ice in Alaska, but there are also swamps, forests, and mountains.

I ride a yellow school bus to get to school. There are roads and cars just like in Tinker Town. I see a lot of moose out the window. They are everywhere!

I miss you too!

Sincerely,

Your friend Ava

Circle the person the class wrote a letter to.

Circle the habitats Ava can see in Alaska.

swamp   mountains   desert

_____

- - - - - - - - - - - - - - - - - - - -

How does Ava get to school? _____

Circle what Ava might wear in the summer.

A **pronoun** is a word that takes the place of a noun.

~~Ava~~ lives in Alaska.

↓

She lives in Alaska.

Fill in the correct pronoun to complete each sentence.

She **Her**

_____ got new warm boots.

They **Them**

_____ like to write.

Me **I**

_____ saw a moose.

Us **We**

_____ miss Ava.

A **determiner** is a word that comes before a noun and gives more information about what the noun is referring to.

> **A** bus was late.

> **This** bus was late.

> **Two** buses were late.

Write the correct determiner to complete each sentence.

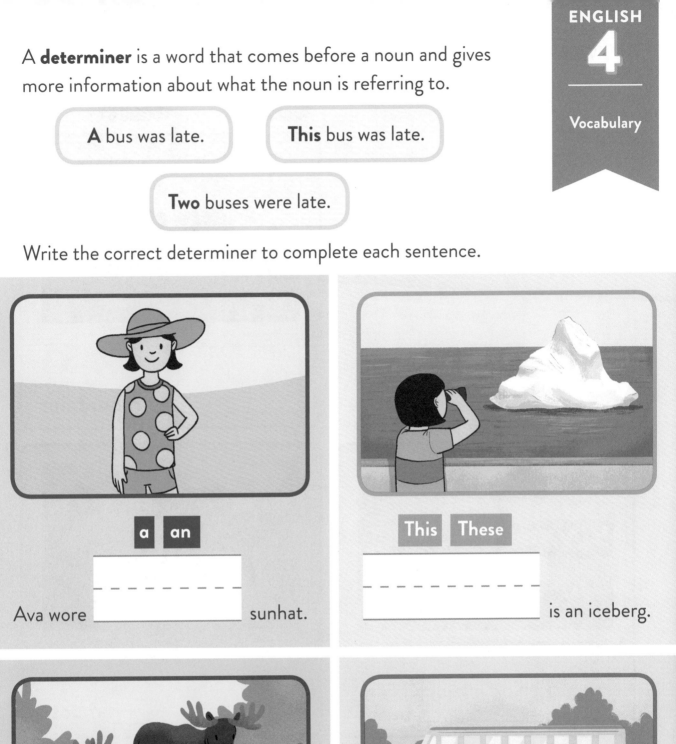

a **an**

Ava wore _____ sunhat.

This **These**

_____ is an iceberg.

That **These**

_____ moose live nearby!

the **an**

Ava takes _____ bus to school!

Write the correct determiner to describe each of Ava's photographs.

one two three four

sun

mountains

buses

moose

icebergs

school

Write your own letter to a friend.

Dear _____,

I live in _____. My home is _____

_____.

To get to school I _____.

Here, the weather is _____. I like to wear

_____ and _____.

There are animals near me, too. I see _____ all

the time! My favorite animal to see is _____.

It is very _____. What I like the most about

living here is _____.

　　　　　Sincerely,

　　　　　_____

Copy your letter onto a separate piece of
paper and mail it with the help of an adult.

Items from outside your home, like:
leaves, twigs, flowers, seeds, pinecones

Paper

Glue

Pencil

Markers

Shoebox

Scissors
(with an adult's help)

LET'S TINKER!

What clothes did you wear today for the weather where you live? **Use** the materials to make drawings or models of what you wore. **Describe** each item with pronouns. **Try** using "it," "they," and "them." What color are they? How many do you have? **Use** color and number words to describe your materials.

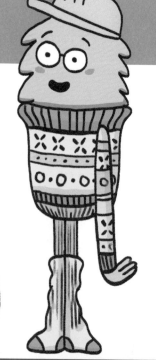

LET'S MAKE: COMMUNITY COLLAGE!

1. Gather the items from outside your home.

2. Place the materials onto a piece of paper. **Create** a design that shows something about the place where you live. **Lay** things in rows, in shapes, stacked together, or however you would like.

3. Glue the materials onto the paper once you have an arrangement you like!

What kind of leaves and flowers did you collect? What could grow from the seeds? Do you know the name of each material? If not, **ask** an adult to help you find out about the trees, flowers, and other items in nature near where you live.

LET'S ENGINEER!

A new family just moved into Tinker Town. Callie wants to tell them all about it, but they speak a different language!

How can Callie share details about Tinker Town if she can't talk about it?

Make a diorama in a shoebox about the place where you live to share with a friend or family member. A diorama is a model. It can show what your neighborhood looks like. **Label** important things in your diorama that you want to share.

PROJECT 4: DONE!
Get your sticker!

Word Meanings

A **flyer** is a piece of paper with information about an event, a person, a place, or a thing. Read the flyer aloud.

JOIN THE **DOUGHNUT PARADE** ON SATURDAY

START

END

SCHEDULE OF EVENTS

1:00 Doughnut Parade

2:00 Doughnut Race

3:00 Concert

4:00 Costume Contest

Prepositions are words that can describe where something is located or when something happens.

Read each question and circle the correct answer.

What will happen **before** the Doughnut Race?

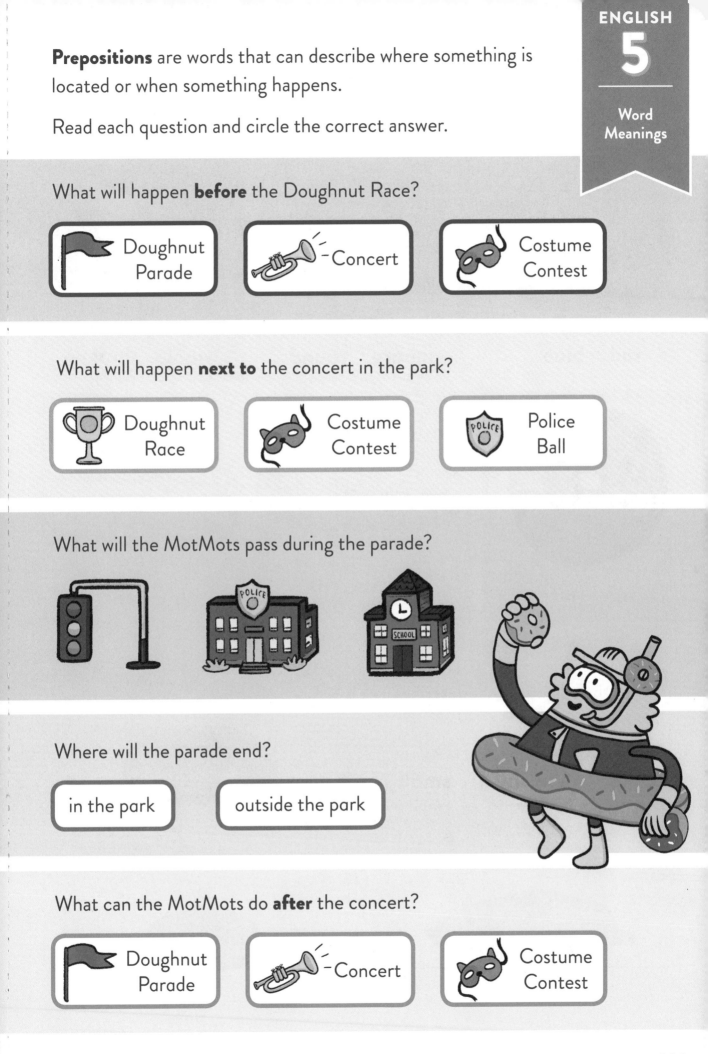

Doughnut Parade

Concert

Costume Contest

What will happen **next to** the concert in the park?

Doughnut Race

Costume Contest

Police Ball

What will the MotMots pass during the parade?

Where will the parade end?

in the park

outside the park

What can the MotMots do **after** the concert?

Doughnut Parade

Concert

Costume Contest

An **adjective** is a word that describes a person, place, or thing. Adjectives can describe color, shape, size, and more!

Circle the adjective that describes each doughnut.

red   blue

square   round

whole   broken

fancy   plain

flat   tall

tiny   large

Write the adjective that describes each doughnut.

hot   mushy   small

Cross out the words that are not adjectives.

colorful

eat

large

sweet

napkin

fresh

yummy

parade

Draw your own doughnut. Then write four adjectives to describe it.

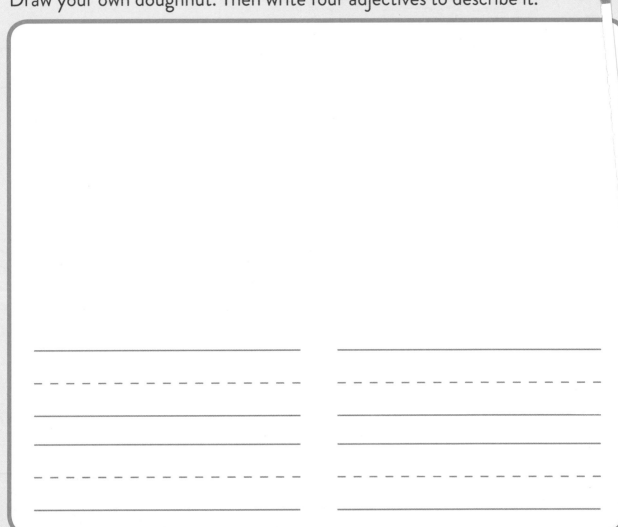

Draw a line to connect each MotMot to the adjective that describes his costume.

silly   fancy   sparkling

Draw your own costume for the Doughnut Parade. Then write three adjectives to describe it.

You can be in the Doughnut Parade, too!
Read each action word, and then act it out.

walk   march   stomp

skip   stroll

Circle the action that made
the most noise with your feet.

What are some other ways you can move in a parade? Draw and write them.

LET'S START!

Empty tissue box

Construction paper

Paper

Glue

Paint

Scissors
(with an adult's help)

Markers

LET'S TINKER!

Find a partner and lay all the materials in front of you. Secretly **choose** a material and describe it to your partner using only adjectives, like descriptions of color, shape, or size. For example, you can say, "I see something red and smooth and flat," to describe red paper. Can your partner guess which object you chose? **Take** turns describing and guessing.

LET'S MAKE: WIGGLE BOX!

1. Decorate an empty tissue box. You can **use** markers, paper, glue, paint, and more.

2. Cut a sheet of paper into 10 pieces.

3. Write an action word on each piece, such as hop, wiggle, gallop, or roar. Then **put** all 10 in the box.

4. Find a partner to play. **Pull** one word from the box and read it aloud. Then **do** the action. For example, if you pull "wiggle," then you wiggle!

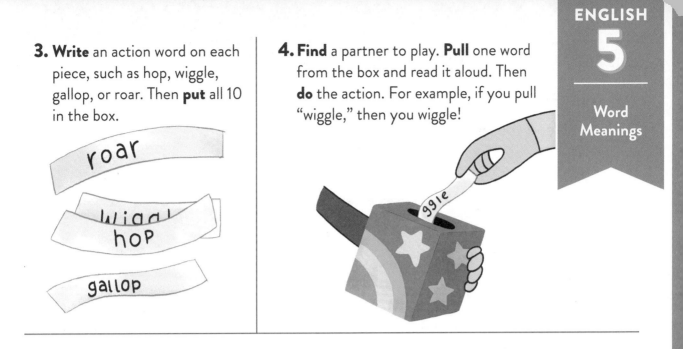

5. Next, your partner **pulls** out a word and reads it. He or she must **do** both actions in order. For example, if your partner pulls out "gallop," first he or she must wiggle, then gallop.

6. Keep going to see who can do the most actions in a row!

LET'S ENGINEER!

The MotMots are throwing a pajama parade and inviting lots of friends.

How can they show or tell their friends where the parade will be?

Make your own pajama parade route and instructions. Will the parade go through your bedroom? Will it start next to your dog's bed? How will you show or tell your friends where it starts and ends?

Pajama Parade ↗

PROJECT 5: DONE!
Get your sticker!

An **essay** is a piece of writing about one specific topic. With the help of an adult, read the essay aloud.

The Flute

I learned to play a new instrument—the flute! It is my favorite instrument. The flute makes a pretty whistling sound. It is called a wind instrument because you can make sounds by blowing air through it.

The flute has three important parts. There is a lip plate at the top. You put your mouth on the lip plate and blow air across a hole. The body of the flute is a long, hollow tube. It is empty inside so it can carry air to the keys. The keys are small metal parts that cover the holes in the body. Each one has a hinge. You can swing them open and closed by pressing with your fingers. That's how you change the sound that comes out of the flute!

The flute is my favorite musical instrument. It is the best because it hums and whistles. I keep mine close to my bed at night. I can't wait to play it again.

Circle the words in the essay that are new to you.

The author wrote that the flute is hollow—it is empty inside.
Circle the object below that is hollow.

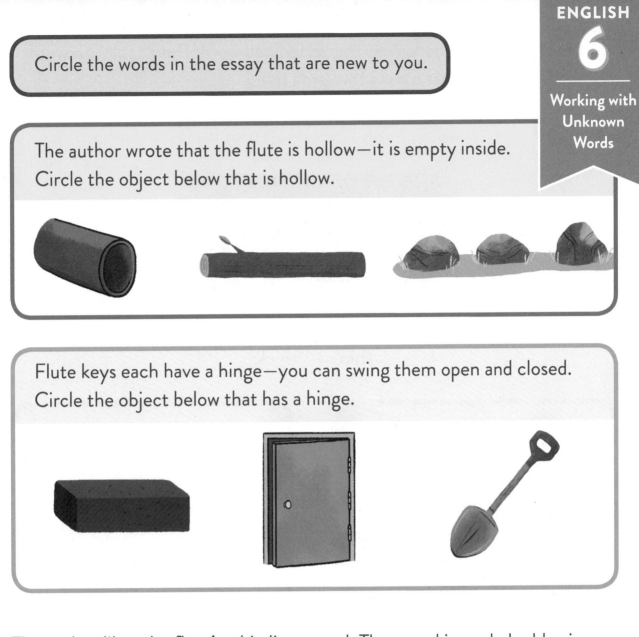

Flute keys each have a hinge—you can swing them open and closed.
Circle the object below that has a hinge.

The author likes the flute's whistling sound. The sound is made by blowing air. Draw a picture of something else that makes a whistling sound.

Read each sentence and look at the underlined word. Then circle the word below the sentence that means the same thing.

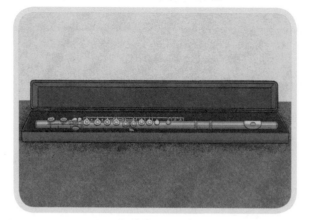

The skinny flute fit into a <u>narrow</u> case.

thin   **thick**

I heard a <u>distant</u> sound from the flute player down the street.

close   **far**

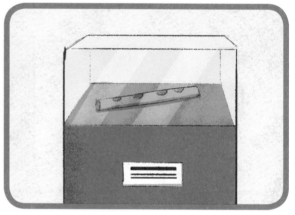

I saw an <u>ancient</u> flute made from a bone in a museum.

old   **new**

The <u>mellow</u> music made me sleepy.

soft   **loud**

No one else was on stage—I played <u>solo</u>.

together   **alone**

A **homograph** is a word that is spelled like another word but that is different in meaning.

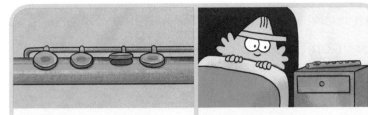

The flute keys open and **close**.

Frank keeps his flute **close** to his bed.

Frank's flute is not heavy. It's **light**.

Circle another meaning of **light**.

Frank hears the bell **ring** at the end of school.

Circle another meaning of **ring**.

Frank **waves** to his flute teacher.

Circle another meaning of **waves**.

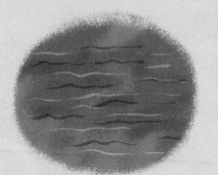

A **conjunction** is a word that joins together two words or phrases. Fill in the missing conjunction to complete each sentence.

Music class is fun _____ we play instruments.

because   or

I tried the trumpet _____ it was hard to play.

but   or

Today I played the flute _____ I tried the drums!

because   and

I want to play the banjo _____ sing in a band.

or   so

I like wind instruments _____ I am learning the flute.

or   so

Complete each sentence.

Dimitri likes to play his sitar alone **but**

_____

_____

_____.

Enid's tuba is big **so** _____

_____

_____

_____.

Amelia can't play her bongos **because**

_____

_____

_____.

LET'S START!

GATHER THESE TOOLS AND MATERIALS.

Jar with a lid

4–6 rubber bands

Tape

4–6 craft sticks

10 or more drinking straws

2 thick books

LET'S TINKER!

Use your materials to make sounds. **Try** tapping, folding, and rubbing them. Can you make sounds like these?

> click   buzz   snap

What are other words that describe the sounds you hear?

LET'S MAKE: TINY BANJO!

1. Wrap 4 thin rubber bands around a jar lid. (If the rubber bands are loose, you can **wrap** them around twice so they are tighter.)

2. Tape them down on the flat back.

3. Tape a craft stick to the flat back as a handle.

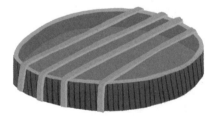

4. Pluck the strings to make music. **Describe** the sounds you make! And **sing** along!

LET'S ENGINEER!

The MotMots took a shortcut to the playground, and there is a river they can't get across! But Enid realizes that a bridge works just like a conjunction—it joins together two places!

How can they build a bridge over the river to get to the playground?

Place two thick books on a table and leave room for your hand in between them. Then **make** a bridge using your materials. Can you get it to go from one book to the other? **Try** making a bigger space between the books, enough for two hands. How long can you make your bridge between the books?

PROJECT 6: DONE!
Get your sticker!

Reading Literature

A **fairy tale** is a story about magical characters, settings, and events that aren't real. With the help of an adult, read this fairy tale aloud.

Jack and the Beanstalk

Once upon a time a boy named Jack lived in a cottage with his mother. They needed money for food, so Jack's mother told him to sell their only cow. On the way to town Jack ran into an old man. "I will trade you your old cow for five magic beans!" the man said. Jack took the magic beans and ran home proudly. But instead of being happy, his mother was angry. She turned bright red and said, "Now we have only five beans and no cow!" Then she threw the beans out the window.

Overnight the beans grew and grew and grew. When Jack awoke, the beanstalk reached the sky! He jumped out of bed and started climbing the beanstalk. He climbed above his cottage and above the clouds, and he saw a shimmering castle. Inside he saw gold coins all around.

Suddenly a giant came into the room. He boomed, "Fee-fi-fo-fum! I see you, you better run!" Jack started running. The giant chased him around the castle! But Jack was too fast for the giant. He hid and the giant sat down and took a nap. Jack quietly grabbed a bag of gold coins and climbed down the beanstalk. He gave the coins to his mother, and she was happy.

Later on, Jack and his mother needed more money for food. So Jack climbed the beanstalk and went to the castle. The giant was there, napping again. Jack grabbed a magical goose and a golden harp. He began to climb down the beanstalk, but the harp made a noise. The giant woke up and boomed, "Fee-fi-fo-fum! I see you, you better run!" Jack climbed down as fast as he could. The giant chased him down the beanstalk, but Jack was still too fast. He jumped to the ground, grabbed an ax, and chopped down the beanstalk. The giant fell to the ground, and the beanstalk fell on top of him. Jack and his mother lived happily ever after.

The end.

What did Jack trade to get the magic beans?

_____

Circle the picture of how Jack's mother felt when he brought home beans.

Circle all the items Jack took from the castle.

What did Jack do with the ax? _____

_____

Stories like fairy tales have settings, characters, and events.

A **setting** is a place in a story.

Draw a picture of what you think these settings may have looked like.

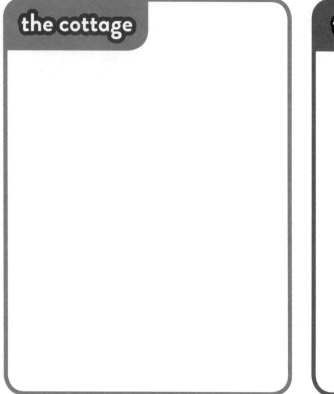

the cottage

the castle

A **character** is a person or animal in a story.

Draw a picture of what you think these characters may have looked like.

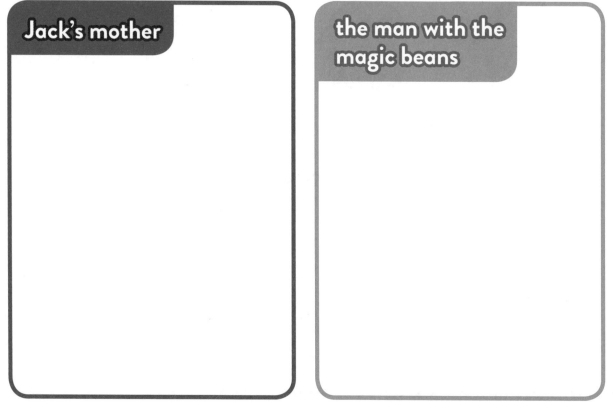

Jack's mother

the man with the
magic beans

Jack

the giant

Circle two adjectives
that describe Jack.

fast   **small**

angry   **giant**

Circle two adjectives
that describe the giant.

large   **happy**

sleepy   **tiny**

Complete the sentence.

Jack climbed up the beanstalk

because _____

_____

_____

_____ .

Complete the sentence.

The giant climbed down the

beanstalk because _____

_____

_____

_____ .

Write how each character may have felt during each event in the story. Then act out the events!

proud   **angry**

Jack feels

_____.

Jack's mother feels

_____.

mad   **scared**

Jack feels

_____.

The giant feels

_____.

worried   **confident**

Jack feels

_____.

The giant feels

_____.

Write the numbers 1, 2, 3, 4, and 5 to put these events from "Jack and the Beanstalk" in order from first to last.

LET'S START!

GATHER THESE TOOLS AND MATERIALS.

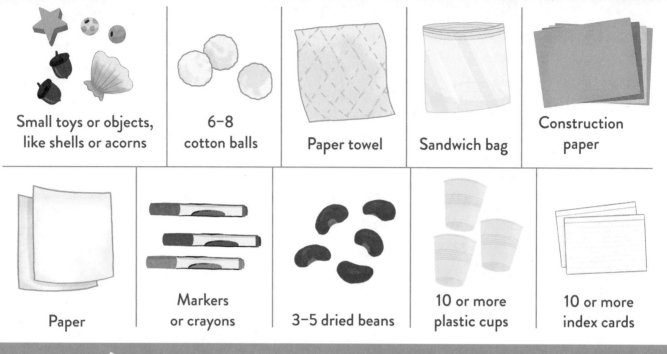

Small toys or objects, like shells or acorns	6–8 cotton balls	Paper towel	Sandwich bag	Construction paper
Paper	Markers or crayons	3–5 dried beans	10 or more plastic cups	10 or more index cards

LET'S TINKER!

In the fairy tale, Jack climbed up into the clouds and found a castle. **Make** your own cloud out of your materials. Which are soft and fluffy? What is hidden in your cloud? **Use** your materials to hide some treasure!

LET'S MAKE: MAGIC BEANS!

1. Fold a wet paper towel and place it inside a sandwich bag.

2. Place a few dried beans inside. You can **use** any beans, like black beans, pinto beans, or kidney beans. **Make sure** the beans are on top of the paper towel, so you can see them.

3. Close the sandwich bag and place it by a window.

4. Watch your beans for a week. What happens inside the bag?

5. Plant your seeds in the dirt if you want to watch them keep growing.

LET'S ENGINEER!

The MotMots read the story "Jack and the Beanstalk." They don't have any magic beans or giant beanstalks, but they would like to climb above the clouds.

How can the MotMots reach the clouds?

Build your own model of a beanstalk. How can you stack your materials to build a taller and taller stalk? How can you combine the materials so the stalk is taller? Can you build as high as your waist, your shoulders, or even the clouds?

PROJECT 7: DONE!
Get your sticker!

A **biography** is a story about a person's life, written by someone else. With the help of an adult, read this biography aloud.

Zaha Hadid

Zaha Hadid was born in Baghdad, Iraq, on October 31, 1930. In school she studied math and science. Then she became an architect. An architect is a person who designs buildings, bridges, and other structures.

Her designs were unique. They didn't look like any other buildings. Some had curved walls and wavy roofs. Some others looked like things in nature—one building was shaped like stones in a river.

Many people said that her unique buildings couldn't be built. They thought it would be too hard. But Zaha believed in her ideas. She kept drawing and designing.

Many years later, Zaha built her first building—a fire station. Then she built another building, and another. Soon she had buildings all over the world! She won awards that women had never won before.

Zaha never stopped believing in her designs. She did what she loved, no matter what people said. Her buildings show her brave ideas and determination.

opera house

art gallery

fire station

bridge

apartment building

You can learn new information from text and from pictures. Write a ✔ next to how you learned each of these facts about Zaha and her buildings.

Zaha was born in Iraq.

☐ text

☐ pictures

She studied math and science.

☐ text

☐ pictures

Zaha designed a bridge shaped like waves.

☐ text

☐ pictures

She won awards that women had never won before.

☐ text

☐ pictures

Some people thought her designs couldn't be built.

☐ text

☐ pictures

Answer each question according to the biography on page 314.

Did Zaha Hadid write this biography?

☐ yes

☐ no

What is an architect?

_____

_____

Circle Zaha's first building.

fire station   opera house   art gallery

What happened after many years that let Zaha know that believing in her ideas had worked?

☐ She studied math and science.

☐ She won awards that women had never won before.

☐ She designed a building with curved walls.

Circle a word that describes Zaha.

determined   bored   lazy

There are many words to describe Zaha's designs. Hunt around your home to find other objects that fit these descriptions. Then draw a picture of each one you find.

pointy

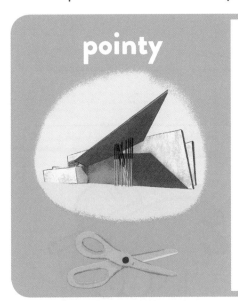

round

wavy

Zaha studied math and science in school so she could become an architect. Write about your favorite thing to study.

_____

_____

Zaha designed some buildings to look like things in nature, like stones, rivers, and sand. Look out your window or go outside. Draw one thing that you see in nature. Then label it.

_____

Draw a picture of your own building design that looks like what you saw outside.

Zaha kept designing buildings even when other people didn't believe in her designs or didn't want to build them. She was determined.

Write about and draw a time that you were determined. Describe something that you kept trying even when it wasn't easy.

_____

_____

_____

_____

_____

LET'S START!

GATHER THESE TOOLS AND MATERIALS.

Small cardboard box	Sandwich bag	6–8 bendable straws	6 or more craft sticks
Tape	Paper	Markers	Scissors (with an adult's help)	Cereal box

LET'S TINKER!

Look at the boxes and bags that your materials came in. What can you learn from the text? What about from the pictures? **Make** a new box or bag for one of your materials. **Draw** and write what you think should be on the package.

LET'S MAKE: BRIDGE CHALLENGE!

1. Cut a half-inch slit in the bottom of a bendable straw.

2. Get another bendable straw and stick the bottom of it into the slit of your first straw.

3. Repeat steps 1 and 2 with another 2 straws.

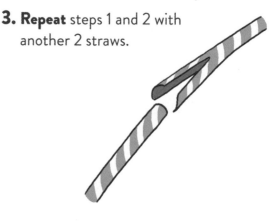

4. Tape 6 craft sticks together in a row.

5. Tape the straws to the craft sticks.

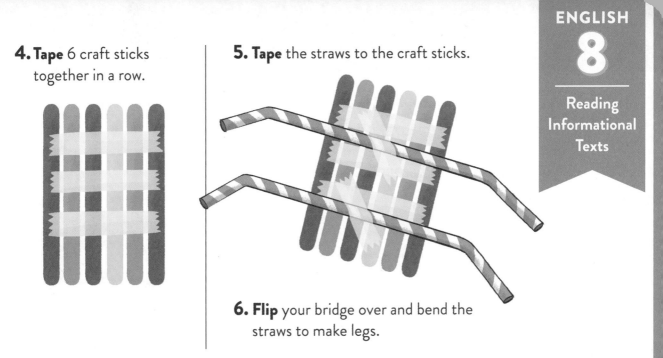

6. Flip your bridge over and bend the straws to make legs.

7. If your bridge is wobbly, **add** another set of straws to strengthen it. You can also **add** tape "feet" to secure the bridge to a surface, like a table.

8. Test your design like an architect. What can it hold on top? What would make it stronger?

LET'S ENGINEER!

Tinker Town needs a new fire station. The town is holding a competition for building designs. The building must be tall, strong, and large enough to fit three fire trucks. Each of the MotMots is planning a design.

How can each MotMot show his or her design to enter the competition?

Draw, build, make a model, or write about your own plan for a Tinker Town fire station. What shape will your design be? How tall can you make it? How will people know that it is a fire station? How can you share your ideas and design?

PROJECT 8: DONE!
Get your sticker!

A **fantasy story** is a fictional text that often includes wizards, monsters, magic, and other supernatural people, places, and things.

With the help of an adult, read each fantasy story aloud.

My First Flying Lesson

My dad gave me my first flying lesson today. He said, "Wing, think about the air rushing past you." I did. He told me to close my eyes. I did. He told me to get a running start and then fly. I ran! But I didn't fly.

Then I saw my friend Racer zoom by. He made flying look easy. I didn't want to move my wings because I was sad. But I tried again anyway. I flapped my wings, but nothing happened. I flapped them faster, but still nothing happened. Tomorrow I will try again. Flying is hard!

Learning to Fly

Hi, my name is Racer!

A few hours ago, I learned to fly! My mom took me outside for a lesson. I couldn't wait to begin—I knew just what I wanted to do.

First, I took a deep breath.

Next, I looked right and left to make sure that the air was clear.

Then, I flapped my wings as fast as I could.

Last, I kicked my feet off the ground, and I flew!

Flying is easy! It's fast and it's fun. Tomorrow I will try flying backward. Maybe I can fly upside down!

Draw a line to connect each quote from the story to the character who said it.

Flying is easy!

I flapped my wings, but nothing happened.

Tomorrow I will try flying backward.

I kicked my feet off the ground, and I flew!

Flying is hard!

Maybe I can fly upside down!

My dad gave me my first flying lesson today.

Compare the two characters from the stories, Wing and Racer.

WING

Write about and draw what happened during Wing's flying lesson.

Write about and draw what Wing thinks about flying.

Write about and draw what Wing will do tomorrow.

Write about and draw one way that Wing and Racer are the same.

What steps did Wing take to try to fly? Act it out!

ENGLISH

9

Comparing Texts

RACER

Write about and draw what happened during Racer's flying lesson.

Write about and draw what Racer thinks about flying.

Write about and draw what Racer will do tomorrow.

Write about and draw one way that Wing and Racer are different.

What steps did Racer take to try to fly? Act it out!

Some texts tell stories, while other texts give information.

Read the diagram to learn information about dragonflies.

Parts of a Dragonfly

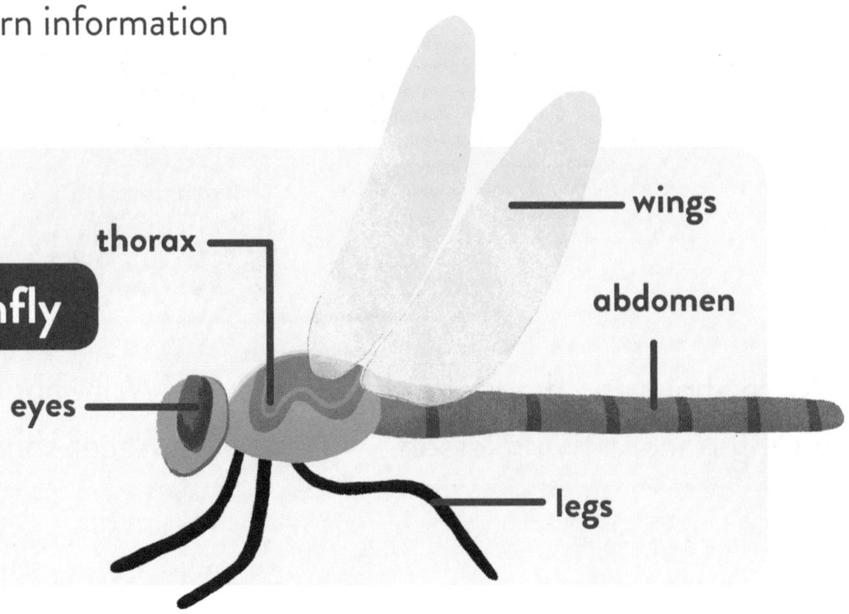

thorax

wings

abdomen

eyes

legs

Write something you learned about dragonflies.

_____

_____

_____

Write about and draw one thing you'd still like to learn about dragonflies.

_____

_____

_____

Look at the picture.

Write and draw your own story about the dragons above.

_____

_____

_____

_____

LET'S START!

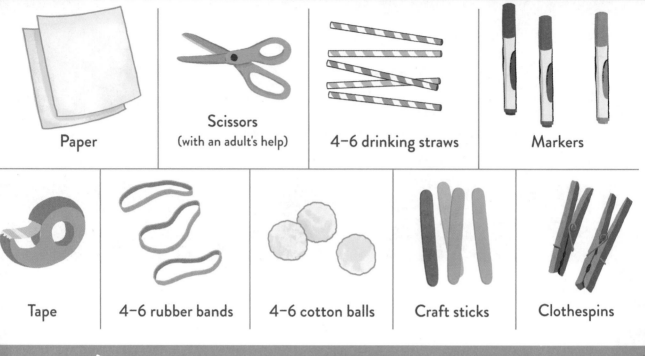

Paper

Scissors
(with an adult's help)

4–6 drinking straws

Markers

Tape

4–6 rubber bands

4–6 cotton balls

Craft sticks

Clothespins

LET'S TINKER!

Choose one of your materials. First, **say** one piece of information about it. Then **tell** one story about it! **Tell** a second story. How were they the same? How were they different?

LET'S MAKE: FLYING DRAGONFLY!

1. Cut a small square piece of paper, about the size of the palm of your hand.

2. Roll the paper around the end of a straw and tape it.

3. Fold over the end of the paper and tape it down.

4. Use a sticker from page 389 to add a dragonfly, another insect, or a fantasy animal.

5. Blow on the straw to watch your animal fly!

LET'S ENGINEER!

The MotMots are entering the Tinker Town Flying Cotton Ball Competition. Each MotMot designs a launcher. Then a cotton ball is pulled back and released to see who is the winner!

How can Frank send his cotton ball the farthest?

Send your own cotton balls flying with a rubber band around your pointer finger. How can you create a design to send your cotton ball farther? Does it matter if your finger is straight or bent? Do any rubber bands work better than others? What materials could work instead of a finger? **Compare** your designs.

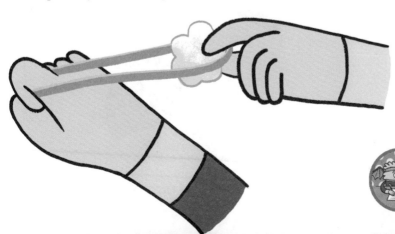

PROJECT 9: DONE!
Get your sticker!

A **play** is a story acted out by actors, sometimes on a stage. The actors read their parts of the play from a **script**. With the help of an adult, read the script aloud.

The Flying Turtle

TURTLE: I want to see the world! But my legs are short. And my home is stuck on my back. So, I can't walk very fast.

DUCK: Maybe we can help you.

(The duck talks to his friend. They pick up a stick.)

DUCK: My friend and I will take you up into the sky! You can see the world. But you must promise not to say one word while we are flying.

TURTLE: Yes! I promise! Let's go!

DUCK: Okay. Bite this stick. Hold tight. And do not say one word!

(The ducks each take one end of the stick. The turtle bites the middle. They fly up in the sky. After a while, they pass a man below on the ground.)

MAN: What a sight! I have never seen a turtle fly!

TURTLE: Hello there!

(As soon as the turtle opens his mouth, he begins to fall . . .)

Write a line that each character may have said after the turtle fell, and read it aloud.

Write about and draw how you think the play ends.

Read each of the turtle's lines below aloud. Look at his face to read the line with the correct expression.

"I want to see the world! But my legs are short. And my home is stuck on my back."

"Yes! I promise! Let's go!"

Read the duck's lines below aloud. Then draw a picture of what you think he may have looked like when he said each one.

"My friend and I will take you up into the sky!"

"Bite this stick. Hold tight."

Read the play on page 330 aloud by yourself or with a partner. Try using different voices for the characters.

Draw a line through the maze to all the places the turtle may have seen on his flight with the ducks.

Circle what the turtle wanted.

to have a stick   **to see the world**   **to make friends**

Why couldn't the turtle see the world? _____

_____

Circle the character who said, "You must promise not to say one word while we are flying."

Why did he say this? _____

_____

What lesson do you think the turtle learned?

Write and draw to retell the play *The Flying Turtle*. What happened first, next, and last?

First, _____

_____

_____

_____

Next, _____

_____

_____

Last, _____

_____

_____

_____

Use your fingers to retell the story, too! Point to your pinkie finger and tell what happens first. Use your other fingers to tell the next events. Then use your thumb to tell what happens last.

LET'S START!

GATHER THESE TOOLS AND MATERIALS.

6 or more small round stones | Glue | Paint | Paintbrush

Markers | A few small paper bags | 3–5 craft sticks | 3–5 cotton balls

LET'S TINKER!

Imagine that your materials have voices. What would each sound like? What might they say? Can you make up a different voice for each material?

Life is Hard!

LET'S MAKE: TURTLE TOY!

1. Find 6 smooth round stones—1 large stone and 5 small stones.

2. Arrange your stones like a turtle: Lay your largest stone down—it will be a turtle shell. **Push** 5 stones under it to be 4 legs and a head.

3. Lift the shell stone and add a large drop of glue to the top of the 5 smaller stones. Then **press** the shell stone down on top.

4. Leave the turtle to dry for several hours.

5. Paint your turtle.

6. Act out your own turtle story! What does your turtle want? What stands in his or her way? How does he or she overcome that obstacle?

LET'S ENGINEER!

Brian and Enid are putting on a play about a turtle who wants to make new friends. He meets a lot of new animals along the way!

How can they make characters to tell their story?

Make characters for your own story with the materials. You can **add** stickers from page 389. Will you make animals, people, or something else— like robots or talking caterpillars? What story can you act out with your characters?

PROJECT 10: DONE!
Get your sticker!

Punctuation

Read the class trip form below. Trace the punctuation at the end of each sentence.

TINKER TOWN SCHOOL

We are taking a class trip to the Statue of Liberty!

The trip will be on April 4th.

The teachers on the trip will be
Mr. Game and Mrs. Play.

WEAR COMFORTABLE SHOES.
We will climb 354 steps to the top of the statue!

WHO IS GOING ON THE TRIP?

My full name is __Greg Thinker_____.

My birth date is __March 15, 2013_____.

My teacher's name is __Mrs. Play_____.

My three favorite trip snacks are __apples, crackers,__

__and nuts_____.

Bring your binoculars.
The Statue of Liberty's torch
is over 305 feet high!

Every sentence has a punctuation mark at the end, like the following.

● A **period** is used at the end of a statement. A statement tells you something.

❓ A **question mark** is used to ask a question.

❗ An **exclamation point** is used to share a big feeling, like excitement.

Read each sentence. Then write the correct punctuation mark at the end.

This is my first trip to New York City____

How long will it take to get there____

The Statue of Liberty is near Ellis Island____

This is the best trip I've ever taken____

Is the Statue of Liberty taller than my home____

I am so excited to climb to the top____

The names of days and months should be capitalized. Write each date with a capital letter.

The trip is in _____.

april

It is on a _____.

saturday

The Statue of Liberty holds a tablet that says _____.

july 4, 1776

The names of specific people should be capitalized. Write each name with a capital letter at the beginning of each word.

_____ and _____ are going on the class trip.

callie   **frank**

The Statue of Liberty is nicknamed _____.

lady liberty

The students will go with _____ and _____.

mr. game

mrs. play

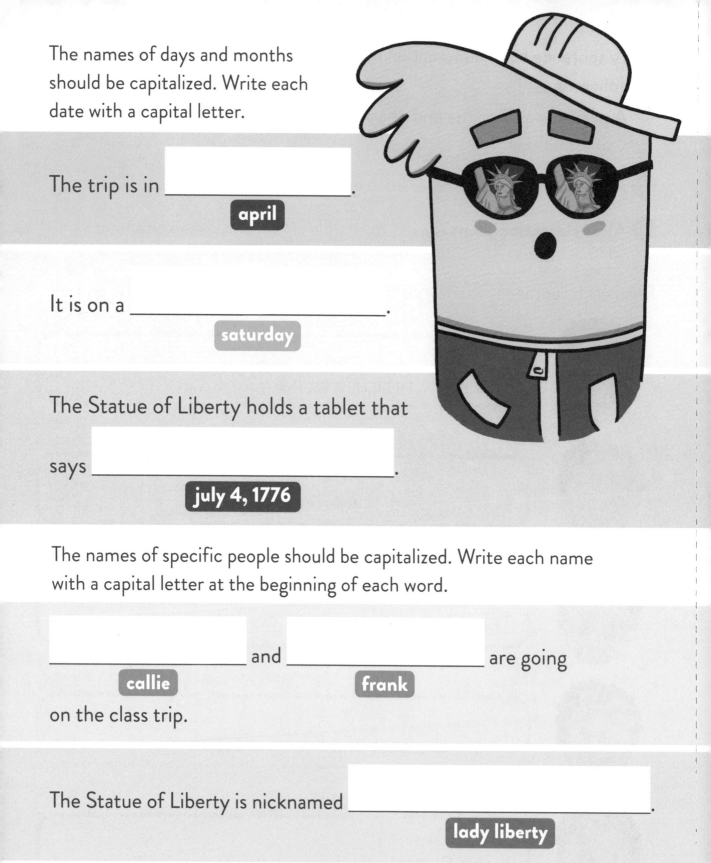

A **comma** is used to separate groups of three or more items in a sentence.

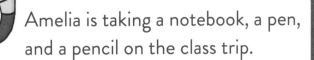

Amelia is taking a notebook, a pen, and a pencil on the class trip.

Complete each sentence with the missing words and necessary commas. Include "and" before the last item.

Callie is taking _____

_____.

a pear   a strawberry   a banana

Enid is taking _____

_____.

a helicopter   a truck   a boat

Frank is taking _____

_____.

a hamburger   a pickle   a hot dog

Finish this sentence.

I would take _____.

A **possessive noun** uses an apostrophe (') to show that something belongs to another person or thing.

When one person or thing owns something, add **'s.**

Callie**'s** map

When more than one person or thing owns something, add ' after the last **s.**

the MotMots**'** map

The MotMots have many plans for their trip to New York City. Use an apostrophe to write each possessive noun correctly.

Amelia_____ plan is to draw in her notebook.

Dimitri_____ plan is to take pictures.

Brian_____ plan is to write a postcard.

The teachers_____ plan is busy!

Write a sentence about Enid's plan.

_____

_____

_____

Fill out the form. Use capital letters and punctuation where necessary.

=== **CLASS TRIP!** ===

My full name is _____.

My birth date is _____.

My teacher's name is _____.

My three favorite snacks are _____

_____.

Write about and draw where you want to go on a class trip.

_____

_____

_____

LET'S START!

GATHER THESE TOOLS AND MATERIALS.

2–3 paper plates	Scissors (with an adult's help)	Glue	Crayons	Paper
20 or more dried beans	Egg carton		7 paper or plastic cups	Tape

LET'S TINKER!

Use your materials to make the shape of the following punctuation marks:

a period .   a question mark ?   an exclamation point !

LET'S MAKE: LIBERTY CROWN!

1. Cut around the inside circle of a paper plate.

2. Cut off the bottom of the outer circle to make a crown.

3. Draw lines to divide the leftover circle into 8 pieces and cut them out.

4. Glue 7 of the triangles to the crown, to match the statue's seven rays.

5. Color the crown with crayons.

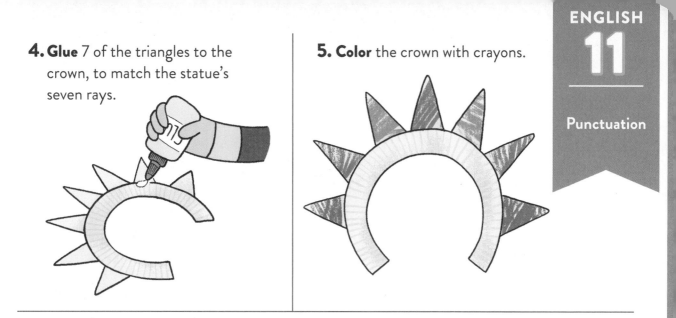

6. Some people think the Statue of Liberty's crown looks like the sun. **Write** a sentence about what you think the crown looks like. Which punctuation mark did you use at the end?

_____

_____

LET'S ENGINEER!

Callie has been saving money for a vacation at Topsy-Turvy Tinker Park. Each ride costs 1 token. She can buy 20 tokens and wants to go on a ride every day for a week.

How can Callie make sure that her tokens last all 7 days?

Use your beans as tokens. How can you sort the beans so there are some for each day? **Try** making a container for each day of the week. **Write** the name of each day of the week on the containers. **Remember** to capitalize them! Does Callie have enough for at least 1 ride per day? How many ways can you sort the beans?

PROJECT 11: DONE!
Get your sticker!

Writing Sentences

With the help of an adult, read the essay aloud.

Dinosaur Fossils

Dinosaurs lived on Earth before people lived on Earth. They are now extinct. That means that there are no dinosaurs alive today.

So how do we know so much about dinosaurs if we never lived with them? We learn about them from the fossils they left behind! People who study fossils are called paleontologists. They find fossils of dinosaur bones, eggs, teeth, and footprints all over the world!

Paleontologists dig for fossils in the ground. They use tools like shovels, axes, and brushes to uncover them. Then they wrap the fossils in plaster. This is so the fossils can be safely moved to labs to be studied. Paleontologists try to figure out what kind of dinosaur each fossil belonged to.

Fossils show that dinosaurs came in all different sizes. Some giants, like Titanosaurus, may have been 130 feet long when they were alive. That's longer than a basketball court! But some other dinosaur fossils are very small. The Microraptor was only a few feet long. It weighed about the same as a chicken.

Dinosaurs were amazing animals. We learn more all the time from studying their fossils. Who knows what we will find out next!

Find an example of each of these types of punctuation in the essay on page 346:

Find an example of each of these types of punctuation in the essay on page 346:

● Draw a ◯ around a period.

❓ Draw a ▢ around a question mark.

❗ Draw a △ around an exclamation mark.

Write the correct punctuation mark at the end of each sentence below.

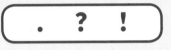

Are there any fossils under my school____

I am so excited to learn about dinosaurs____

Callie-saurus would be a good dinosaur name___

Write one question you have about dinosaurs. Use a capital letter at the beginning of your sentence and a question mark at the end.

_____

_____

Use your finger to draw each type of end punctuation in the air.

Sentences can talk about the past, present, or future.

Write the correct form of each verb in the paleontologists' schedule.

YESTERDAY

I dug.

We _____.

He _____.

They brushed.

I scraped.

We _____.

Write a sentence about each dinosaur and what is happening in each picture. Use a capital letter for the first word of each sentence and a punctuation mark at the end.

Velociraptor

_____

_____

_____

_____

Baryonyx

_____

_____

_____

_____

Titanosaurus

_____

_____

_____

_____

Answer each question with a sentence. Use an "!" at the end of sentences that you are excited about.

What is your favorite animal?

_____

_____

Why is this animal the best?

_____

_____

What is one thing you'd like to learn about this animal?

_____

_____

Draw a picture of yourself with your favorite animal.

LET'S START!

GATHER THESE TOOLS AND MATERIALS.

1 cup flour	1 cup dirt	½ cup sand (or use more dirt)	1 cup water	Spoon	Small plastic toys or real objects that can get wet, like: a shell, an acorn, or a rock
Bowl	Tray	Paper	Pencil	8 or more craft sticks	Glue

LET'S TINKER!

Pick up one of your materials. **Play** with it and describe aloud what you are doing. For example, "I dig in the sand."

Then **say** the sentence again in the past tense, to describe how you would have used it yesterday. For example, "Yesterday I dug in the sand."

Can you say how you would play with each material today and yesterday? What about tomorrow?

LET'S MAKE: TOY FOSSIL DIG!

1. **Mix** the flour, dirt, sand, and 1 cup of water in a bowl.

2. **Stir** it until it's like thick mud. (If it's runny, add more dirt, sand, and flour.)

3. **Grab** a handful of the mud mixture and make a ball around a small toy (or something from outside, like a shell or rock). It will **feel** like making a snowball around your "fossil"! **Try** making several balls, each with a different item inside.

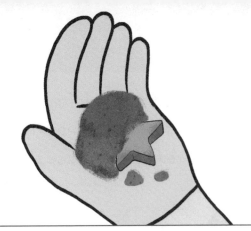

4. **Lay** the mud balls on a tray to dry, either inside or outside in the sun. After a few hours, **flip** them over so that both sides dry.

5. After they have dried overnight, **dig** for your very own fossils using the craft sticks!

LET'S ENGINEER!

Callie took a trip to the dinosaur museum. She saw fossils of bones, footprints, and even dinosaur poop!

How can she share the facts she learned about dinosaurs with her friends?

Make your own dinosaur exhibit with models of fossils. You can **make** eggs, teeth, or even a whole dinosaur. Then **write** labels for your exhibit. You can **share** names and facts, or even ask questions you still have about dinosaurs!

PROJECT 12: DONE!
Get your sticker!

Telling a Story

A **timeline** can be used to share information about an event or a story. It shows the order that things happened from the past to the present. With the help of an adult, read the timeline aloud. Then answer each question.

The First Moon Landing

The Apollo 11 spacecraft launched from Earth into space. Inside were Neil Armstrong, Buzz Aldrin, and Michael Collins.

July 16, 1969

Four days later, Armstrong and Aldrin landed a part of their spacecraft on the moon.

July 20, 1969

Write a ✔ next to the event that happened first.

☐ The Apollo 11 spacecraft launched from Earth.

☐ Armstrong and Aldrin landed a part of their spacecraft on the moon.

Write a ✔ next to the event that happened last.

☐ The astronauts collected moon soil.

☐ The astronauts returned to Earth.

Armstrong opened the hatch, climbed down nine steps, and became the first person to walk on the moon!

Twenty minutes later, Aldrin joined him on the moon. They collected some moon soil to bring back home.

The three astronauts returned safely to Earth. Since then, twenty-one more people have traveled to the moon.

July 21, 1969

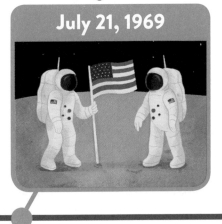

July 21, 1969

July 24, 1969

On what date did the Apollo 11 spacecraft launch into space?

_____

Who took the first steps on the moon?

_____

How many astronauts walked on the moon on July 21, 1969?

_____

What did the astronauts bring back from the moon?

_____

The timeline on pages 354 and 355 tells about an event: the first moon landing. Stories can also tell about events. They can be about your life—events that were happy, important, silly, or more. Everyone has stories to tell!

Write about and draw the first thing you did today.

Where were you?

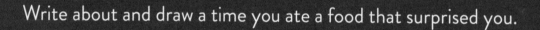

Write about and draw a time you ate a food that surprised you.

What did you say?

Write about and draw a time you went somewhere new.

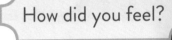

How did you feel?

Write about and draw a time you and your family laughed.

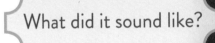

What did it sound like?

The timeline on pages 354 and 355 tells about what happened first, next, and last when Neil Armstrong walked on the moon.

Write and draw your own timeline that tells about an event from your life. Use your writing on pages 356 and 357 for ideas.

Title: _____

First, I _____

_____.

PAST

Next, I _____

_____.

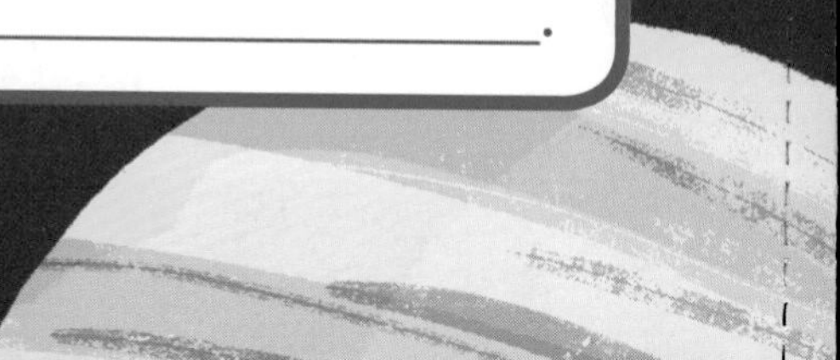

Then, I _____
_____ .

Last, I _____
_____ .

Want to share your story? You can use computers, tablets, phones, and more to send it to friends and family. Ask a friend or an adult to help!

LET'S START! GATHER THESE TOOLS AND MATERIALS.

Pencil	2 toilet paper tubes	Paper towel tube	Small piece of cardboard
Markers or paint	Scissors (with an adult's help)	Paper	Glue

LET'S TINKER!

Think about your favorite memory from your last birthday. What did you do? Who else was there? **Use** your materials to help you act out the story for a friend or family member.

LET'S MAKE: SUPER SPACECRAFT!

1. Lay a toilet paper tube on top of a piece of cardboard. **Trace** it.

2. Draw a rounded nose to the traced shape. Then **draw** two rounded triangles for wings.

3. Cut out shape.

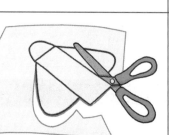

4. With the help of an adult, **trace** the bottom of a toilet paper tube on top of another. Then **cut** out the round shape.

5. Glue your cut tube on top of the cardboard in the shape of a spacecraft, and let it dry.

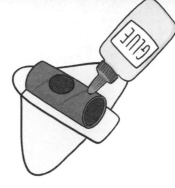

6. Color or paint your spacecraft. You can also **decorate** it with stickers from page 389.

7. Place a small toy inside and go for a ride. **Tell** a story about where you're going!

LET'S ENGINEER!

Callie is thinking about her last birthday. She remembers seeing friends, blowing up balloons, and opening presents. But she can't remember what she did first or last in the day.

How can she put the events of her birthday in order?

Make your own timeline of your last birthday. **Use** the materials to write about and draw what you did first, next, and last. How can you connect them so they stay in order, like a timeline?

PROJECT 13: DONE!
Get your sticker!

With the help of an adult, read this informational text aloud.

Glowing Animals

Many animals use special body parts to help them survive. Some deep-sea animals glow! It's called bioluminescence. These animals have organs that create and shine light.

Anglerfish have a long piece of fin that extends over their heads like a fishing pole. An organ on the end glows. Other fish swim close thinking the light is a snack, but they become dinner for the anglerfish instead.

Atolla jellyfish have red bodies with many tentacles. When they are in danger, they light up a bright blue ring to scare predators! They have been nicknamed "alarm jellyfish" for how they glow to stay safe.

Cockatoo squid have transparent bodies. They are almost completely see-through, which is great camouflage. They have glowing lights under their eyes to help hide their dark eyeballs from predators, too.

Circle the animal that is almost completely transparent.

Draw a picture of the animal with tentacles.

Circle the part of the anglerfish that glows.

Draw lines to match each animal with the reason why it uses bioluminescence.

to attract prey to eat

to scare predators away

to hide from predators

Many other kinds of animals use their special parts to help them survive. Read about each animal and answer the questions.

WOODPECKERS
have sticky tongues.

CHAMELEONS
have very fast tongues.

GIRAFFES
have long tongues.

Which of these animals do you think reaches far away for food?

_____

Why? _____

_____

Which of these animals do you think catches food that's moving quickly?

_____

Why? _____

_____

PORCUPINES
have sharp quills.

TURTLES
have heavy and hard shells.

ARMADILLOS
have tough plates of armor.

Which of these animals do you think is too slow to run from danger?

_____

Why? _____

_____

Which of these animals do you think can poke a predator?

_____

Why? _____

_____

Hunt around the inside and outside of your home. Write about and draw the animals that you see.

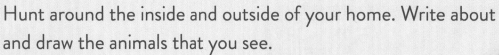

Circle any special body parts that help these animals survive.

Write facts about your favorite animal that you saw.

Animal's name: _____

Does it live inside or outside? _____

How does it move? _____

_____

Does it live alone or with other animals? _____

_____

Why is it your favorite animal that you saw? _____

_____

Write and draw other facts you know about this animal.

Is it fast or slow? How does it protect itself? Can it fly? How many legs does it have? What does it eat?

Modeling clay	2 or more clothespins	Plastic cup	String	Scissors (with an adult's help)
4–6 beads or buttons	Markers	Paper	Tape	

LET'S TINKER!

Make a model of your favorite animal with the materials. What shape is it? How big or small is it? Does it swim or fly? What body parts can you make?

LET'S MAKE: ANGLERFISH GAME!

1. With the help of an adult, **use** scissors to poke a small hole in the center of the bottom of a plastic cup.

2. **Cut** a 12-inch piece of string. **Thread** one end of the string through the bottom of the cup. **Use** a piece of tape in the bottom of the cup to stick it in place.

3. Tie a bead (or button) to the other end of the string. If the bead is very small, **tie** on a few more.

4. Use paper and a marker to add eyes and teeth to your cup so it looks like a fish.

5. Hold the cup in your hand. **Flip** the bead in the air and catch it in the cup, just like an anglerfish catching prey in its jaws.

LET'S ENGINEER!

The MotMots are on an animal safari in the park. They love the sandwiches that Dimitri packed for their picnic lunch. They want to be able to make the sandwiches themselves!

How can Dimitri share the recipe for his special sandwiches?

Write and draw your own instructions about how to make your favorite sandwich or snack. What ingredients and tools do you need? What do you do first? Next? And last? **Try** reading your instructions to a family member. **Ask** him or her to make your recipe using your instructions to see if they work!

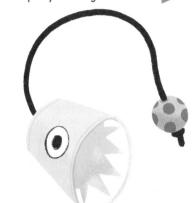

PROJECT 14: DONE!
Get your sticker!

Research to Gain Understanding

A **cinquain poem** has five lines that follow a special pattern. Read the cinquain poem aloud.

At Night

by Cora

Bedtime
Dark, quiet
Reading, resting, thinking
Happy in my bed
Sleep

A **free verse poem** has no patterns or rules. Read the free verse poem aloud.

Dark Night

by Eli

So black.
I can't see anything.
It's time to go to bed.
BUT.
I'm scared!
Too much fear to fall asleep.
I wish I had a light.
A bright spot for the dark night.

Write and draw research questions about the poems.

? What is one thing you wonder about Cora's bedtime?

What question do you have for Cora about feeling happy?

? What is one thing you wonder about Eli's bedtime?

What question do you have for Eli about feeling scared?

Write what you think Cora and Eli would say if you asked them these questions.

Poems express thoughts and feelings. Write sentences and draw some of your thoughts and feelings.

My name: _____

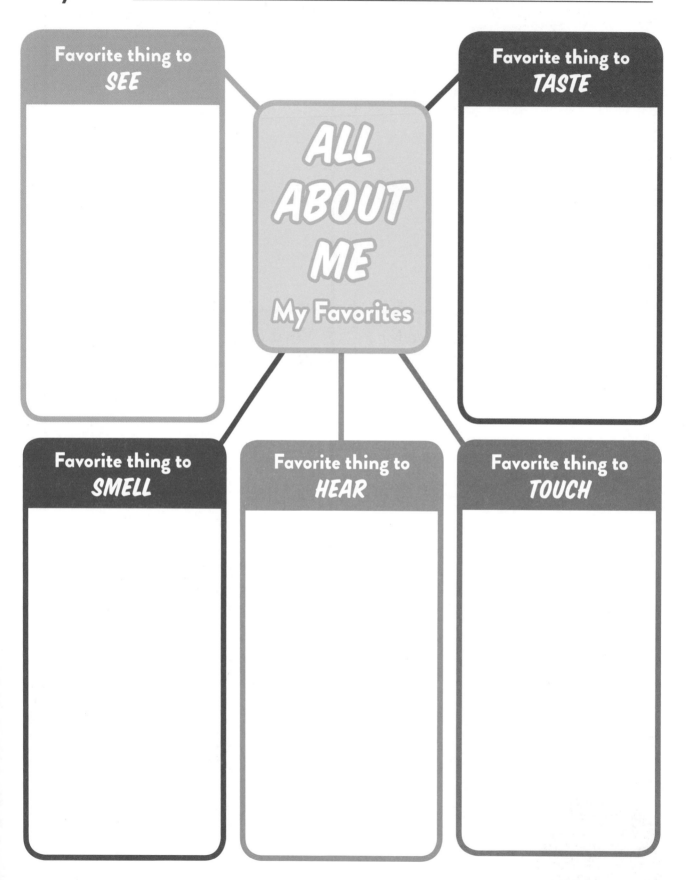

Favorite thing to **SEE**

Favorite thing to **TASTE**

ALL ABOUT ME My Favorites

Favorite thing to **SMELL**

Favorite thing to **HEAR**

Favorite thing to **TOUCH**

Write about and draw something that makes you feel:

excited

nervous

brave

cheerful

curious

silly

A cinquain poem always has five lines that follow a special pattern.

My Pet ← title

Cat ← topic

Soft, fluffy ← adjectives that describe the topic

Petting, purring, playing ← verbs, action words

Nervous he'll scratch me ← a phrase about feelings

Friend ← describes the topic

Write your own cinquain poem about one of your favorite things. Look at your research on pages 372 and 373 for ideas of what to write about.

_____

_____, _____

_____, _____, _____

_____

_____

Use the research you've gathered from pages 372 and 373 to write your own free verse poem. Write about your favorites, memories, or even write made-up stories.

GATHER THESE TOOLS AND MATERIALS.

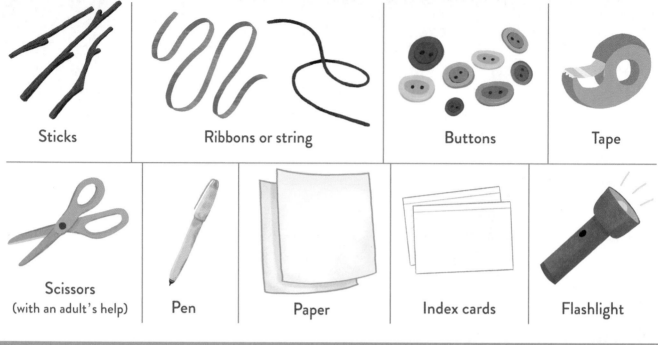

Sticks	Ribbons or string	Buttons	Tape
Scissors (with an adult's help)	Pen	Paper	Index cards	Flashlight

LET'S TINKER!

Research how light and dark affect these materials. **Turn** a light on and off. How do they look? **Go** outside. Do they look different in the sun? **Try** the flashlight, too. Which can you see the best in the dark?

LET'S MAKE: STORY STICK!

1. **Decorate** your stick with your choice of ribbons, string, buttons, and tape.

2. **Find** one partner (or more!) to start the game.

3. Hold the story stick. **Say** one sentence to start a story. For example, "The monster walked to the park."

4. Pass the stick to the next person. Now they **continue** the story by saying one sentence about what happens next. For example, "When the monster got to the park, he went on a swing!"

5. Pass the stick until everyone has had one turn. Then it's your turn again. **Keep passing** the stick and taking turns until the story is done.

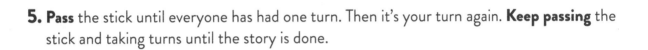

LET'S ENGINEER!

Callie is afraid of the dark. She wants to know if her friends are, too, so they can help each other feel better.

How can she find out how her friends feel about the dark?

Ask your friends and family members questions about the dark. What questions will you ask to learn how they feel? Then **make** something to help someone who is afraid of the dark. **Try** making a night-light, a poem, or even a dream catcher. Which do you think would help? **Ask** questions to find out!

PROJECT 15: DONE!
Get your sticker!

ANSWER KEY

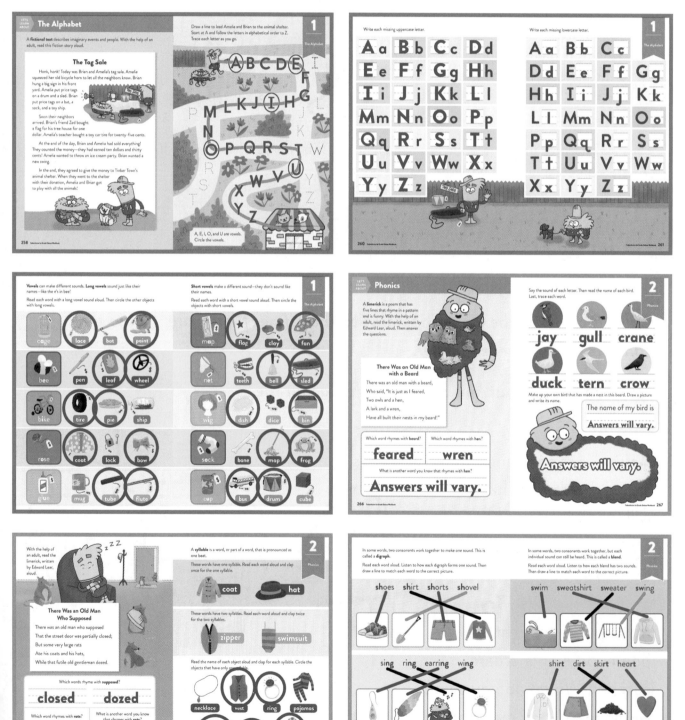

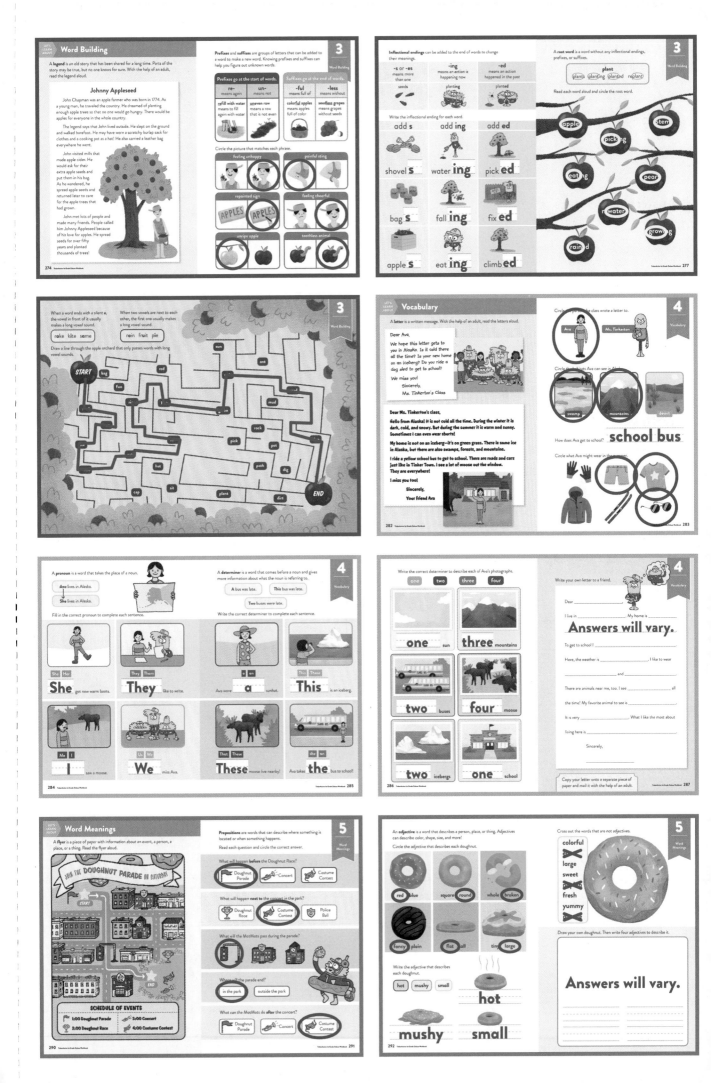

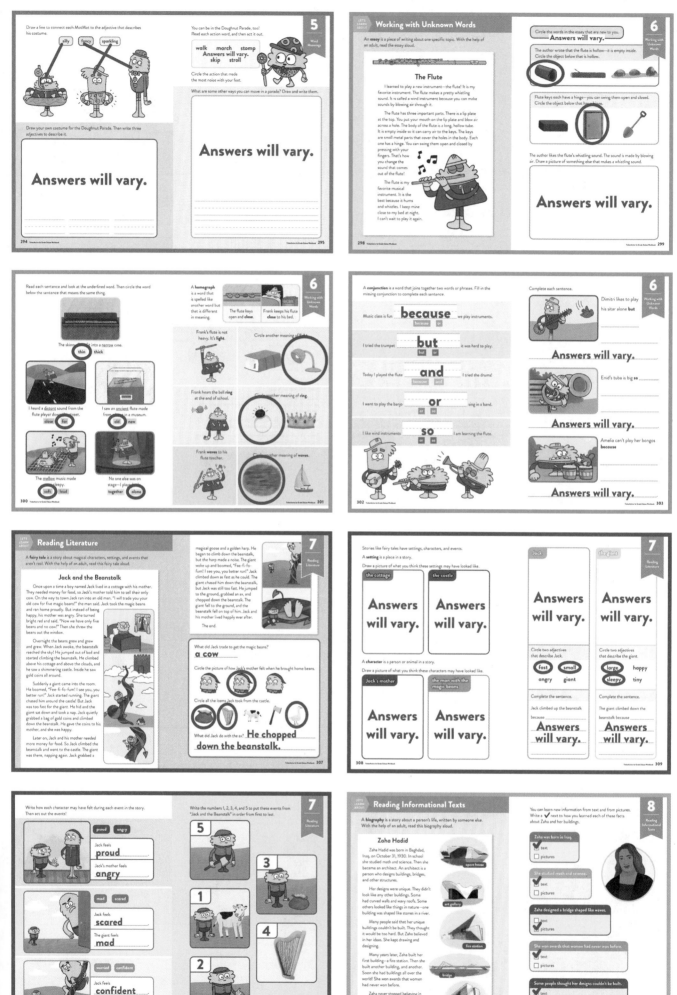

Draw a line to connect each MotMot to the adjective that describes his costume.

silly   fancy   sparkling

Draw your own costume for the Doughnut Parade. Then write three adjectives to describe it.

Answers will vary.

You can be in the Doughnut Parade, too! Read each action word, and then act it out.

walk   march   stomp
Answers will vary.
skip   stroll

Circle the action that made the most noise with your feet.

What are some ways you can move in a parade? Draw and write them.

Answers will vary.

6

Working with Unknown Words

An **essay** is a piece of writing about one specific topic. With the help of an adult, read the essay aloud.

The Flute

I learned to play a new instrument—the flute! It is my favorite instrument. The flute makes a pretty whistling sound. It is called a wind instrument because you can make sounds by blowing air through it.

The flute has three important parts. There is a lip plate at the top. You put your mouth on the lip plate and blow air across a hole. The body of the flute is a long, hollow tube. It is empty inside so it can carry air to the keys. The keys are small metal parts that cover the holes in the body. Each one has a hinge. You can swing them open and closed by pressing with your fingers. That's how you change the sound that comes out of the flute!

The flute is my favorite musical instrument. It is the best because it hums and whistles. I keep mine close to my bed at night. I can't wait to play it again.

Circle the words in the essay that are new to you.
Answers will vary.

The author wrote that the flute is hollow—it is empty inside. Circle the object below that is hollow.

Flute keys each have a hinge—you can swing them open and closed. Circle the object below that has a hinge.

The author likes the flute's whistling sound. The sound is made by blowing air. Draw a picture of something else that makes a whistling sound.

Answers will vary.

Read each sentence and look at the underlined word. Then circle the word below the sentence that means the same thing.

The skinny flute fit into a narrow case.
thin   thick

I heard a distant sound from the flute player down the street.
close   far

I saw an ancient flute made from bone in a museum.
old   new

The mellow music made me sleepy.
soft   loud

No one else was on stage—I played alone.
together   alone

A **homograph** is a word that is spelled like another word but that is different in meaning.

The flute keys open and close. Frank keeps his flute close to his bed.

Frank's flute is not heavy. It's light.
Circle another meaning of light.

Frank hears the bell ring at the end of school.
Circle another meaning of ring.

Frank waves to his flute teacher.
Circle another meaning of waves.

A **conjunction** is a word that joins two words or phrases. Fill in the missing conjunction to complete each sentence.

Music class is fun **because** we play instruments.
because   or

I tried the trumpet **but** it was hard to play.
but   or

Today I played the flute **and** I tried the drums!
because   and

I want to play the banjo **or** sing in a band.
or   so

I like wind instruments **so** I am learning the flute.
or   so

Complete each sentence.

Dimitri likes to play his sitar alone but

Answers will vary.

Enid's tuba is big so

Answers will vary.

Amelia can't play her bongos because

Answers will vary.

7

Reading Literature

A **fairy tale** is a story about magical characters, settings, and events that aren't real. With the help of an adult, read this fairy tale aloud.

Jack and the Beanstalk

Once upon a time a boy named Jack lived in a cottage with his mother. They needed money for food, so Jack's mother told him to sell their only cow. On the way to town Jack ran into an old man. "I will trade you your old cow for five magic beans!" the man said. Jack took the magic beans and ran home proudly. But instead of being happy, his mother was angry. She turned bright red and said, "Now we have only five beans and no cow!" Then she threw the beans out the window.

Overnight the beans grew and grew and grew. When Jack awoke, the beanstalk reached the sky! He jumped out of bed and started climbing the beanstalk. He climbed above his cottage and above the clouds, and he saw a shimmering castle. Inside he saw gold coins all around.

Suddenly a giant came into the room. Ha boomed, "Fee-fi-fo-fum!" Jack started running. The giant chased him around the castle! But Jack was too fast for the giant. He hid and the giant sat down and took a nap. Jack quietly grabbed a bag of gold coins and climbed down the beanstalk. He gave the coins to his mother, and she was happy.

Later on, Jack and his mother needed more money for food. So Jack climbed the beanstalk and went to the castle. The giant was there, napping again. Jack grabbed a magical goose and a golden harp. He began to climb down the beanstalk, but the harp made a noise. The giant woke up and boomed, "Fee-fi-fo-fum! I see you, you better run!" Jack climbed down as fast as he could. The giant chased him down the beanstalk, but Jack was still too fast. He jumped to the ground, grabbed an ax, and chopped down the beanstalk. The giant fell to the ground, and the beanstalk fell on top of him. Jack and his mother lived happily ever after.

The end.

What did Jack trade to get the magic beans?
a cow

Circle the picture of how Jack's mother felt when he brought home beans.

Circle all the items Jack took from the castle.

What did Jack do with the ax? He chopped down the beanstalk.

Stories like fairy tales have settings, characters, and events.
A **setting** is a place in a story.
Draw a picture of what you think these settings may have looked like.

the cottage
Answers will vary.

the castle
Answers will vary.

A **character** is a person or animal in a story.
Draw a picture of what you think these characters may have looked like.

Jack's mother
Answers will vary.

the man with the magic beans
Answers will vary.

Jack
Answers will vary.

the giant
Answers will vary.

Circle two adjectives that describe Jack.
fast   small
angry   giant

Circle two adjectives that describe the giant.
large   happy
sleepy   tiny

Complete the sentence.
Jack climbed up the beanstalk because
Answers will vary.

Complete the sentence.
The giant climbed down the beanstalk because
Answers will vary.

Write how each character may have felt during each event in the story. Then act out the events!

proud   angry
Jack feels proud
Jack's mother feels angry

mad   scared
Jack feels scared
The giant feels mad

worried   confident
Jack feels confident
The giant feels worried

Write the numbers 1, 2, 3, 4, and 5 to put these events from "Jack and the Beanstalk" in order from first to last.

5
3
1
4
2

Reading Informational Texts

A **biography** is a story about a person's life, written by someone else. With the help of an adult, read this biography aloud.

Zaha Hadid

Zaha Hadid was born in Baghdad, Iraq, on October 31, 1930. In school she studied math and science. Then she became an architect. An architect is a person who designs buildings, bridges, and other structures.

Her designs were unique. They didn't look like any other buildings. Some had curved walls and wavy roofs. Some others looked like things in nature—one building was shaped like stones in a river.

Many people said that her unique buildings couldn't be built. They thought it would be too hard. But Zaha believed in her ideas. She kept drawing and designing.

Many years later, Zaha built her first building—a fire station. Then she built another building, and another. Soon she had buildings all over the world! She won awards that women had never won before.

Zaha never stopped believing in her designs. She did what she loved, no matter what people said. Her buildings show her brave ideas and determination.

opera house
art gallery
fire station
bridge
apartment building

You can learn new information from text and from pictures. Write a ✔ next to how you learned each of these facts about Zaha and her buildings.

Zaha was born in Iraq.
✔ text
☐ pictures

She studied math and science.
✔ text
☐ pictures

Zaha designed a bridge shaped like waves.
☐ text
✔ pictures

She won awards that women had never won before.
✔ text
☐ pictures

Some people thought her designs couldn't be built.
✔ text
☐ pictures

Answer each question according to the biography on page 314.

Did Zaha Hadid write this biography?
☐ yes
☑ no

BIOGRAPHY OF ZAHA HADID

What is an architect?
An architect is a person who designs buildings, bridges, and other structures.

Circle Zaha's first building.
(fire station) / opera house / art gallery

What happened after many years that let Zaha know that believing in her ideas had worked?
☐ She studied math and science.
☑ She won awards that women had never won before.
☐ She designed a building with curved walls.

Circle a word that describes Zaha.
(determined) / bored / lazy

There are many words to describe Zaha's designs. Hunt around your home to find other objects that fit these descriptions. Then draw a picture of each one you find.

pointy — Answers will vary.
round — Answers will vary.
wavy — Answers will vary.

Zaha studied math and science in school so she could become an architect. Write about your favorite thing to study.
Answers will vary.

Zaha designed some buildings to look like things in nature, like stones, rivers, and sand. Look out your window or go outside. Draw one thing that you see in nature. Then label it.
Answers will vary.

Draw a picture of your own building design that looks like what you saw outside.
Answers will vary.

Zaha kept designing buildings even when other people didn't believe in her designs or didn't want to build them. She was determined.

Write about and draw a time that you were determined. Describe something that you kept trying even when it wasn't easy.
Answers will vary.

Comparing Texts

A **fantasy story** is a fictional text that often includes wizards, monsters, magic, and other supernatural people, places, and things.

With the help of an adult, read each fantasy story aloud.

My First Flying Lesson

My dad gave me my first flying lesson today. He said, "Wing, think about the air rushing past you." I did. He told me to close my eyes. I did. He told me to get a running start and then fly. I ran! But I didn't fly.

Then I saw my friend Racer zoom by. He made flying look easy. I didn't want to move my wings because I was sad. But I tried again anyway. I flapped my wings, but nothing happened. I flapped them faster, but still nothing happened. Tomorrow I will try again. Flying is hard!

Learning to Fly

Hi, my name is Racer!

A few hours ago, I learned to fly! My mom took me outside for a lesson. I couldn't wait to begin—I knew just what I wanted to do.

First, I took a deep breath.

Next, I looked right and left to make sure that the air was clear.

Then, I flapped my wings as fast as I could.

Last, I kicked my feet off the ground, and I flew!

Flying is easy! It's fast and it's fun. Tomorrow I will try flying backward. Maybe I can fly upside down!

Draw a line to connect each quote from the story to the character who said it.

- Flying is easy!
- I flapped my wings, but nothing happened.
- Tomorrow I will try flying backward.
- I kicked my feet off the ground, and I flew!
- Flying is hard!
- Maybe I can fly upside down!
- My dad gave me my first flying lesson today.

WING / RACER

Compare the two characters from the stories, Wing and Racer.

WING

Write about and draw what happened during Wing's flying lesson.
Answers will vary.

Write about and draw what Wing thinks about flying.
Answers will vary.

Write about and draw what Wing will do tomorrow.
Wing will try flying again.

Write about and draw one way that Wing and Racer are the same.
Answers will vary.

What steps did Wing take to try to fly? Act it out!

RACER

Write about and draw what happened during Racer's flying lesson.
Answers will vary.

Write about and draw what Racer thinks about flying.
Answers will vary.

Write about and draw what Racer will do tomorrow.
Racer will try flying backwards.

Write about and draw one way that Wing and Racer are different.
Answers will vary.

What steps did Racer take to try to fly? Act it out!

Some texts tell stories, while other texts give information.

Read the diagram to learn information about dragonflies.

Parts of a Dragonfly
thorax, wings, abdomen, eyes, legs

Write something you learned about dragonflies.
Answers will vary.

Write about and draw one thing you'd still like to learn about dragonflies.
Answers will vary.

Look at the picture.

Write and draw your own story about the dragons above.
Answers will vary.

Reading Comprehension

A **play** is a story acted out by actors, sometimes on a stage. The actors read their parts of the play from a **script**. With the help of an adult, read the script aloud.

The Flying Turtle

TURTLE: I want to see the world! But my legs are short. And my home is stuck on my back. So, I can't walk very fast.

DUCK: Maybe we can help you.

(The duck talks to his friend. They pick up a stick.)

DUCK: My friend and I will take you up into the sky! You can see the world. But you must promise not to say one word while we are flying.

TURTLE: Yes! I promise! Let's go!

DUCK: Okay. Bite this stick. Hold tight. And do not say one word!

(The ducks each take one end of the stick. The turtle bites the middle. They fly up in the sky. After a while, they pass a man below on the ground.)

MAN: What a sight! I have never seen a turtle fly!

TURTLE: Hello there!

(As soon as the turtle opens his mouth, he begins to fall . . .)

Write a line that each character may have said after the turtle fell, and read it aloud.
Answers will vary.
Answers will vary.

Write about and draw how you think the play ends.
Answers will vary.

Read each of the turtle's lines below aloud. Look at his face to read the line with the correct expression.

"I want to see the world! But my legs are short. And my home is stuck on my back."

"Yes! I promise! Let's go!"

Read the duck's lines below aloud. Then draw a picture of what you think he may have looked like when he said each one.
Answers will vary.
Answers will vary.

"My friend and I will take you up into the sky!"

"Bite this stick. Hold tight."

Read the play on page 330 aloud by yourself or with a partner. Try using different voices for the characters.

Draw a line through the maze to all the places the turtle may have seen on his flight with the ducks.
Answers will vary.

Circle what the turtle wanted.
to have a stick / (to see the world) / to make friends

Why couldn't the turtle see the world? **Because the turtle's legs are short and its home is stuck on its back.**

Circle the character who said, "You must promise not to say one word while we are flying."
(duck circled)

Why did he say this? **So the turtle didn't fall from the stick.**

What lesson do you think the turtle learned?
Answers will vary.

Write and draw to retell the play The Flying Turtle. What happened first, next, and last?

First, Answers will vary.

Next, Answers will vary.

Last, Answers will vary.

Use your fingers to retell the story, too! Point to your pinkie finger and tell what happens first. Use your other fingers to tell the next events. Then use your thumb to tell what happens last.

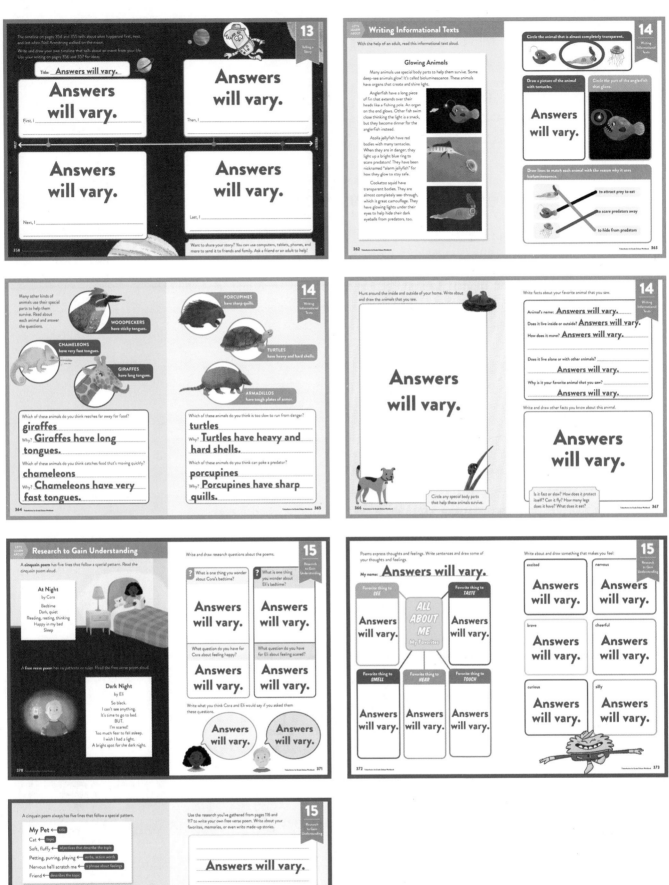

Odd Dot
120 Broadway
New York, NY 10271
OddDot.com

ISBN: 978-1-250-88473-2

WRITERS   Justin Krasner and Megan Hewes Butler
ILLUSTRATORS   Chad Thomas, Lauren Pettapiece, Les McClaine, and Taryn Johnson
EDUCATIONAL CONSULTANTS   Amanda Raupe and Mindy Yip
CHARACTER DESIGNER   Anna-Maria Jung
LEAD SERIES DESIGNER   Carolyn Bahar
INTERIOR DESIGNERS   Phil Conigliaro and Tim Hall
COVER DESIGNER   Caitlyn Hunter
EDITORS   Justin Krasner and Nathalie Le Du

Our books may be purchased in bulk for promotional, educational, or business use. Please contact your local bookseller or the Macmillan Corporate and Premium Sales Department at (800) 221-7945 ext. 5442 or by email at MacmillanSpecialMarkets@macmillan.com.

DISCLAIMER
The publisher and authors disclaim responsibility for any loss, injury, or damages
that may result from a reader engaging in the activities described in this book.

TinkerActive is a trademark of Odd Dot.
Printed in China by Dream Colour (Hong Kong) Printing Limited, Guangdong Province
First published for special markets in 2020
First trade edition, 2023

10   9   8   7   6   5   4   3   2   1